Eat Me Now!

Healthy Macrobiotic Cooking for Students and Busy People

By

Melanie Brown Waxman

Foreword by Michio Kushi

PublishAmerica
Baltimore

ISBN: 1-4241-9173-4 (softcover)
ISBN: 978-1-4489-0714-4 (hardcover)
PUBLISHED BY PUBLISHAMERICA, LLLP
www.publishamerica.com
Baltimore

Printed in the United States of America

To my beautiful, smart, and talented children,
Alisa, Madeline, Amy, Zoe, Andrew, Natasha and Sam…
I love you with all my heart.

I give my deepest appreciation to Michio Kushi and his late wife, Aveline, for their incredible dedication to the macrobiotic movement. I give thanks to my big brother, Simon Brown and my greatest friend, Helen Stevenson; who are always there for me, and my beautiful and supportive family; my late father, Michael; my mother, Patsy, and Dragana, Christopher, Alexander, Nicholas, and Michael Brown; and, my lovely brother, Adam, and his wife, Angela, and Francesca and Georgina. I give many blessings to my extended family: Denny, Joe, Naomi, Nathan, Marina, Susan, and Judy Waxman. Also, my very special friends; Brett Salmon, Michael Kessler, Ryan Kelly, Gabor Szalontay, Brandon Emery, Juan Buritica, Reggie Adams, Gary Miller, Jamie Trevena; and my co-workers at Avante Salon and Spa. To Kayla Evan, Terri Remedio, and Kim Pickett who have given me so much support on my journey; and my cooking group: Maria, Barb, Melissa, Patti, Carol and Cheryl. To all the macrobiotic teachers in the world, a huge, 'thank you', for sharing your lives and working so hard for one peaceful world, and a big blessing to the on line macro group and my massage and cooking clients. Lastly, I would like to give thanks to Megan Cittadino for her wonderful illustrations, artistic advice, and enthusiasm and to Publish America for making this book possible

Table of Contents

Symbols for making the best recipe choice
S = Simple
A = Adventurous
V = Vegan
ST = Strengthening
R = Relaxing
C = Cleansing
E = Energizing

Foreword by Michio Kushi

When I came to America in 1949, I had the vision and dream to create a peaceful world through the practice of macrobiotics and healthy eating. At that time, there was neither an organic nor a natural foods movement. Together with my wife Aveline, I started small classes in New York and Boston and attracted a group of young Hippies who were also looking for a way to spread peace in the world. My idea was to start a grass roots movement that could be built from the ground up through students, individuals, families, and local communities. The first step was to talk to local farmers and ask them to start growing organic food. We even offered to buy all the produce if they couldn't sell it. I also encouraged my students to start natural food processing and learn how to make foods like miso, tofu, shoyu, and sourdough bread, and to harvest sea vegetables. This was the beginning of the natural foods movement that is a thriving and accepted way of living and eating today.

Organic food has now become a huge, national business enterprise. In 2002, the National Organic Standards, which were backed by the US government, went into effect. This has made certified organic foods available in almost every food store and supermarket throughout America.

In the 1980's, macrobiotics gained notoriety as a cancer prevention diet and people slowly began to question the relationship between food and health. Today, macrobiotics is rapidly becoming known as the ultimate healthy diet and has started to appeal to all segments of society. Hotel chains like the Ritz Carlton, Westin, and Prince Hotels serve macrobiotic meals in their restaurants. Today, many doctors, healthcare professionals, business people, Hollywood movie stars, sports stars, and even those in the White House are incorporating macrobiotic dishes—wholly or in part—into their diets.

In 1993, new dietary guidelines were issued by the US government that moved broadly in a macrobiotic dietary direction, suggesting that Americans use plant foods as a foundation for their meals. The American Heart Association has also endorsed balanced vegetarian meals as healthful and nutritionally sufficient.

The macrobiotic movement started because we lived by example. We turned a dream into reality through the practical application of cooking whole, living foods. My early students were very energetic and enthusiastic. As they changed their diet, they started to look great, recover from various physical ailments, and generally felt more happy and peaceful. This had an incredible effect on their friends and family who also wanted to learn their secrets for staying healthy and looking younger. Macrobiotic centers grew up in many cities throughout the United States and classes and seminars were offered which helped to develop a broad base of like-minded people. In 1999, The Smithsonian Institute opened the Michio Kushi Family Collection on Macrobiotic and Alternative Health Care at the National Museum of American History in Washington DC. This collection recognizes macrobiotics as the spearhead for the natural foods, holistic health, and alternative medicine movements in America.

Sadly, at the same time that this incredible movement was taking hold, another trend was creating a huge change in the general eating patterns in the world. More and more people are using packaged, processed, and refined items, which has caused an equally considerable decline in the health of society. We still live in a world where there are wars, poverty, global warming, and many increasing health problems. So in spite of everything, we have a great deal of work to do in order for this world to become peaceful and healthy.

I am so happy that Melanie has written this cookbook because the key to regaining the health of our planet begins in the kitchen, preparing organic, wholesome, nutritious meals. I first met Melanie in Belgium in the early '80s when she was in her 20s. Over the years, she has become an eloquent and lively macrobiotic teacher and cook. She is the mother of seven strong and independent children and yet her youthful attitude continues to shine through. I hope that you can embrace macrobiotics with the help of the delicious recipes in this book. Straightforward as it may seem, the transformation that macrobiotic cooking and eating can bring to you, your family, and friends will have a deep and lasting effect on our world.

In Peace
Michio Kushi
Brookline, MA
August 2007

Introduction by Melanie

Eat Me Now!; is drawn from my experience as a mom of seven children; an artist and a lover of nature and animals; and as a result of helping many people transform their diet and lifestyle. It is packed with easy to follow, practical suggestions and recipes that I have used everyday in our home. I encourage you to view the foods and ideas with an open mind and be alert for the potential for greater health. You can be your own warrior and choose the speed at which you desire to change. Even the smallest shift can be huge on the road towards health, happiness, and adventure.

Many times we feel we cannot make a difference in the world and that the problems are too great. Any change begins with a thought and when that thought becomes action, great things can happen. Even a simple choice to eat whole grains or cut back on animal food has a huge effect. If everyone decided to buy organic foods and do simple things to protect the environment, the world would quickly become a very different place. It is important to understand that what you do everyday does make a difference. There are many examples of how swiftly things take hold in society. I remember in the early eighties, when I was working for the Financial Times, the first word processors came out. They were huge and kept in a special room. We could only work on them for half an hour at a time because they were considered bad for your health. Today most people have a computer system in their homes. We can see how quickly fashions take hold. A hip cell phone or a new style of boots comes out and soon they are all the rage and everyone wants them. What you do today will affect you, your friends, family, community, and your world tomorrow. Even a few encouraging words can help transform a life. It is important to understand that you can—and do!—make a difference.

My journey began in the sunny English countryside. I rode horses, participated actively in the social scene, and obsessed about my weight. I never had a weight problem, but became preoccupied with fashion magazines, looking really thin and becoming a model. I started experimenting with various diets at the age of sixteen. I loved food so could never quite commit to one diet for long enough. I was fortunate to be blessed with robust health; otherwise I would have felt much worse than I did. I flip-flopped between eating apples, yogurt, and diet coke for days and then marvelous home-cooked meals with plenty of desserts when I couldn't resist any longer. As a result my life was a series of ups and downs and most of the time I hated how I looked and felt, which affected my energy, emotions, and outlook.

I first heard of macrobiotics at the age of twelve when my mother ate a macrobiotic meal prepared by the son of one of her friends. I was horrified to hear that she ate seaweed despite her attempt to convince me that it actually tasted pretty good. I then dabbled with eating brown rice when I was 16 after reading an ancient book on macrobiotics. My feeble attempt lasted three days when I gave in to some delicious looking cookies, infinitely tastier than the three small bowls of brown rice I had eaten in an effort to cleanse my system.

I actually started macrobiotics in full force when I was twenty one. Ironically the son who had cooked for my mother became my boyfriend. My parents were appalled because Pat had the reputation of being somewhat outrageous. He was intense, energetic, and passionate about macrobiotics, having eaten grains, beans, and veggies since the early '70s. This was pretty far out for the British but extremely appealing to a somewhat rebellious twenty year old. He told me I would never have to worry about my weight if I ate macrobiotics. That was all I needed to hear and I was willing to have a go even if the food tasted terrible. Fortunately, Pat was an incredible cook and I found the meals absolutely delicious, satisfying, and wholesome.

I was very nervous about cooking myself and could only confidently cook brown rice and sautéed carrots while still enjoying my apples. However I picked up a macrobiotic cookbook by Michel Abeshera and started experimenting. At first, I would only make the dishes with foods I knew and since many of them were unusual, I was rather limited. Then I started using the array of exotic and different ingredients, which made all the difference to the taste and to my energy and health. While I was cooking and eating macrobiotics, something great happened. I started to feel different. I had tons more vitality, felt really positive and joyful and yet also felt peaceful. Every day I rode my bicycle across London to work at the *Financial Times* and would buy hummus and tabouli salad from a little vegetarian restaurant around the corner. I became the all-time macro enthusiast and felt high on life.

As I continued to study and understand more about the philosophy of macrobiotics, I developed an enormous zest for life, which has enabled me to do things that I never imagined possible. I have lived in three countries and met people from all walks of life. My children are strong, independent, and intelligent and add a sparkle to every aspect of my world. Our home is full of fun, adventures, and laughter. Mealtimes are especially lively. We have had lots of other kids come to our house throughout the years and many stayed for dinner. My children used to worry that they would be judged because of the strange food being prepared in our kitchen. Interestingly enough, their friends possessed a wonderful spirit of interest and were pretty much open to anything. Even weird delights were sampled with relish, including sea vegetables, burdock, natto and other strange-sounding (and tasting) delicacies.

After the movie about the pig, *Babe* came out, loads of kids wanted to become vegetarian. Most children had no idea that the meat on their plates came from pigs, chickens, cows or sheep, a reality that is naturally unappealing to most. Unfortunately, many kids opted to eat pizza, chocolate and soda, which are nutritionally deficient and not healthy choices. A vegetarian without veggies is a bit of an irony if you think about it. On the other hand, when you embark on a diet based around whole grains, beans, vegetables, nuts, seeds, and fruit there is an abundance of protein, calcium, iron and all the necessary minerals and vitamins. Not only will you improve your own health, you will be saving the lives of millions of animals and supporting natural and traditional farming methods at the same time.

Making the choice to eat a healthy diet is one of the most solid actions of self-love you can choose. The great thing about nourishing the self is that you also nourish the living world. You are actually taking part in the health and future of the earth in a positive and empowering manner.

For you…healthy foods can help to prevent disease; increase vitality; provide strength; produce strong bones; enhance immunity; and develop creative clear thinking, inner peace, and calm emotions.

For the animals…you participate in the prevention of violence and trauma inherent to meat production and the unnecessary slaughter that occurs today.

For our planet…choosing to eat grains and vegetables is a step towards increasing the chance that our fragile planet will survive and flourish by healing the eco-system and slowing down the vanishing rain forests and dwindling water supplies. And eating a grain-based diet is one of the best ways you can help to stop global warming.

We live in a crazy world of salmonella-tainted chickens, mad cow disease, hormone injected meats, e-coli contaminated spinach, and foods filled with empty calories, additives, and preservatives. The decision to eat a diet of organic, plant-based, living foods is a very sensible one and not as difficult as you may think.

It is time to take a stand and to be pro-active in the nonviolent yet powerful movement towards world peace, the healing of the earth, and evolving into a strong, vibrant, healthy and happy person. It is time to grab this book and begin your journey! I invite you to enjoy *Eat Me Now!*

Many blessings
Melanie

The Ins and Outs of the Macrobiotic Diet

What Does Macrobiotics Mean?

- Macrobiotics comes from the Greek words, *macro* and *bios* meaning large or great life. So when folks say I eat macro food, they are really saying, I eat great food or in the title of this book, macrobiotic recipes really means great life recipes.

- The basis of macrobiotics is that you can achieve the best possible health and make the most of your life by living naturally in harmony with everything around you.

- Macrobiotics is a traditional and natural way of living and eating.

- Macrobiotic foods have been eaten by the worlds healthiest and ancient of cultures. The ingredients are the found in Japanese, Middle Eastern, Indian, Chinese, Eastern European, and Mediterranean cooking among many others.

- The foods come straight from the land or sea and are traditionally prepared rather than being tampered with by highly processed methods of food production.

- There is an emphasis on eating whole, living, foods, which means you get to enjoy the energy of the foods along with all their nutrients. This living energy feeds your own life force and helps you to feel vital, strong, and happy.

- Macrobiotics was once thought of as a cancer prevention diet but is now recognized as an extremely healthy way of eating.

- There are a wide variety of nutritious foods and cooking styles and the approach is flexible, encouraging the development of your creativity and intuition.

- Macrobiotics can be adapted to suit different cultures, climates, and age groups. The dishes taste delicious and are easy to prepare.

- Macrobiotic cooking is a way to find foods that are right for you and to restore a sense of balance to any situation or circumstance.

Why Eat Macrobiotic Food?

- Macrobiotics is a broad, varied, and nourishing diet consisting of grains, beans, sea vegetables, vegetables, seeds, fish, fruit, and various seasonings.

- The diet strengthens the immune system's ability to fight off disease and prevent allergies. The foods keep the immune system healthy and strong and protects against illness.

- Whole foods help you to feel calmer, more relaxed and peaceful, and improve sleep.

- The diet uses organic, living foods that are packed with energy and nutrition.

- It is high in fiber, which is easily absorbed and strengthening, yet gentle on your digestion.

- The diet is good for circulation and keeps the heart strong. It also enhances blood quality and keeps cholesterol levels down.

- The foods help to create strong teeth and bones.

- Macrobiotic ingredients provide a balance of acid and alkaline and sodium and potassium.

- Grains and vegetables are ideal brain food. They help you to concentrate and develop mental clarity.

- The combination of foods provides a balance of protein, iron, calcium and other minerals and vitamins.

- It is a great diet for staying healthy and reduces the risk of cancer and other serious diseases. Studies have found that a plant-based diet helps protect against prostate, colon, skin, and many other types of cancer.

- Macrobiotics keeps you in your skinny jeans; it helps you to maintain your natural weight. Diets that are high in vegetable proteins are much lower in fat and calories.

- Fruits, vegetables, and juices contain phytochemicals that help you to detoxify naturally

- Macrobiotic ingredients have cool colors. The rainbow of colors that we find in fruits and vegetables are produced by phytochemicals. So the yellows, reds, greens and purple's are actually good for your health and boost immunity, prevent infections, and reduce inflammation. The use of color in cooking also stimulates the appetite and makes you feel refreshed and satisfied.

- Macrobiotics saves money. It is possible to eat a whole grain, bean, and vegetable diet and cut down on your food bills.

What About the Protein?

- Many times there is a concern about getting enough protein on a macrobiotic diet. Some people think that you can only get protein from meat and dairy foods. Actually, all natural foods have some protein.

- Vegetables, beans, grains, fish, and nuts all contain ample amounts of protein. These foods are considered to be the mainstays of the macrobiotic diet.

- In order to get enough amino acids (components of protein), it is important to eat a good variety of foods that contain protein such as brown rice served with nuts and beans. A mixture of plant proteins eaten throughout the day will also provide the essential amino acids.

- If you are very active or playing sports, you can have more vegetable quality protein such as beans, tofu, tempeh, seitan, nuts and seeds to maintain your energy levels.

Other Important Nutrients for Students

- Adolescence is an important time for maintaining and building healthy bones and teeth. Bone density is determined in adolescence and young adulthood; so it is essential to include calcium into your diet on a daily basis. The best sources of calcium are unhulled sesame seeds, sea vegetables, green leafy vegetables, fish, and nuts. Other good sources of calcium are toasted sesame butter and orange juice. Sesame seeds contain a rich assortment of minerals including magnesium and copper. This tiny powerhouse of nutrition is excellent for bone development. A teaspoonful of roasted sesame seeds daily is a tasty and nutritional addition to your meals.

- Iron requirements of teenagers and students are relatively high. By eating a varied diet, you can meet your iron needs, while avoiding the excess fat and cholesterol found in red meats. In fact, green leafy vegetables—especially watercress—have three times more iron per calorie than red meat. Dulse (a sea vegetable), pumpkin seeds, sesame seeds, oysters, and lentils are excellent sources of iron. Dishes such as sukiyaki or sautéed carrots cooked in a cast iron skillet can also help to increase your iron intake.

- Vitamin B12 is found in small amounts in fermented foods like miso and tempeh. It is found in much higher amounts in fish and seafood, especially clams and calamari.

- In general, a varied whole grain, bean, and vegetable diet is rich in minerals, vitamins, and antioxidants. It is also high in fiber, which keeps the digestive tract healthy and reduces the risk of cancer. High fiber also moves food through the colon and helps you to have regular and healthy bowl movements.

- Macrobiotic foods are low in the saturated fats that create sticky blood and high cholesterol, although the diet does contain fats that are monounsaturated and polyunsaturated. These fats are vital for good health. It is important to include some fat into your diet in the form of nuts, seeds, beans, and oils. Fish and deep fried foods are extremely beneficial if you are very active and play sports.

Everything Is Energy

One of the main principles of macrobiotics is the understanding that there is a constant flow of universal energy that creates all that we are and see in our physical world. We will take a quick look at how this energy manifests and the ways that we can use it in daily life.

The Yin and Yang of It All

Today the oriental words *Yin* and *Yang* have become trendy terms to describe opposites like woman and man, dark and light, negative and positive, or heads and tails.

In Oriental philosophy, Yin was described as the shady side of the mountain where everything is still, quiet, damp, and peaceful; Yang was described as the sunny side where everything is bright, dry, lively, and active.

The origin of yin and yang comes from the idea that every object in the universe is created by the unique interaction of two opposing energies, which constantly move and flow from one to the other.

Yin is expansive or passive and yang contracted or active.

If we look at the sea, we can see that the waves come in and go out, gently moving back and forth, expanding and contracting. The same goes for breathing. We breathe in and our body expands and breathe out and our body contracts. We only breathe in for so long before we have to change to the opposite and breathe out. The sea can't just come in and we can't only breathe out. There is a continuous dance between the two, back and forth.

Yin and yang are considered polar opposites, yet they constantly interact with each other and are dependant upon each other to exist. Day is yang and night is yin. Day cannot exist without night and night cannot exist without day. There is an uninterrupted flow from one phase to the other and we cannot pinpoint the exact moment when day turns into night or when night becomes day. Yang is summer and yin is winter; south is yang and north is yin. Each pair exists in a state of mutual dependence, and without its opposite it cannot continue.

Nothing is totally created from only yin or only yang. Within Yang there is always a small piece of Yin. Within Yin there is always a small piece of Yang. In the middle of winter, which is yin, a seed, which is yang, lays deep in the ground waiting to become life. In the middle of a boiling hot summer day, which is yang, a sudden rainstorm can bring coolness, which is yin. There are no absolutes, just cycles in time.

You can pretty much classify anything in terms of yin and yang.

Here are some examples:

Yang
- Contracted
- Active
- Short hair
- Male
- Masculine
- Day
- Active
- Sports
- Cycling
- Sun
- Summer

- Warm
- South
- Fire
- Time
- Strong
- Longer, stronger, simple cooking

Yin
- Expanded
- Passive
- Long hair
- Female
- Feminine
- Night
- Passive
- Artistic
- Reading
- Moon
- Winter
- Cool
- North
- Water
- Space
- Gentle
- Quick, lighter, relaxing, more complicated cooking

In day-to-day life, we naturally seek balance and, without knowing it, use yin and yang. We socialize (yang) and sleep (yin). We play sports (yang) and then go on the computer to talk on 'face book' (yin). We eat some salty chips (yang) and drink a large glass of cold water (yin).

We also make balance with our eating and even junk food can be categorized by yin and yang such as eating hamburgers (yang) and ice cream (yin). When compared to other foods, these are considered extremely yang and extremely yin.

The healthier approach is to eat foods that are balanced or middle of the road. Otherwise there is a tendency to swing from one extreme to the other. This yo-yo affect then carries over into other areas of our life. Our emotions, outlook, health and energy levels also go up and down like a roller-coaster ride. If we choose foods that are balanced in terms of yin and yang, then our emotions become calmer, our outlook brighter, and energy steady and enduring.

Foods that have balanced energy are whole, living grains, beans, vegetables, sea vegetables, nuts, seeds, and fruits.

Foods that are extremely yang:
- Hard cheese
- Seafood such as salmon, tuna, swordfish
- Meat
- Chicken
- Eggs
- Salty foods like corn chips
- Tobacco
- Refined salt

Foods that are extremely yin:
- Milk
- Alcohol
- Honey and sugar
- Ice cream
- Drugs (like LSD, cocaine, marijuana)
- Genetically modified foods
- Coffee
- Spices
- Stimulants
- Medications (such as aspirin)
- Tropical vegetables and fruits
- Refined foods like white flour
- Most food additives of a chemical nature

Moderate and more balanced foods (these are classified from more yang at the top to more yin at the bottom):
- Sea salt
- Miso and shoyu
- White fish (more moderate than dark-flesh fish)
- Sea vegetables
- Whole cereal grains
- Beans and bean products
- Vegetables
- Seeds
- Nuts
- Temperate fruits (such as apples, pears, and berries)
- Unrefined oils such as sesame, olive and safflower
- Amasake
- Grain sweeteners such as rice syrup
- Kukicha tea
- Spring water

Yang Produce:
- Grow downward and inward such as root vegetables
- Have a warming effect on the body
- Are heavier and more dense such as root vegetables
- Red, orange, yellow, and brown in color such as squash, carrots, burdock
- Have low water content such as grains and beans
- Have a bitter or salty taste such as miso, shoyu, and seeds
- Grow in colder climates such as buckwheat.

Yin Produce:
- Grow upward and outward such as leafy greens
- Have a cooling effect on the body
- Are lighter and more porous such as lettuce
- Violet, blue, green, and white in color such as grapes, leafy greens, and leeks
- Have higher water content such as melons and cucumber.
- Have a sweet or sour taste such as lemons, syrups, and fruit.
- Grow in warmer climates such as tropical fruit

Everything in nature has specific qualities, which make them more yin or yang. We can use different characteristics to help us to decide which foods are yin or yang.

All things have varying degrees of yin and yang. You need to look at the predominant characteristics in order to discover if something is more yin or more yang:

- A parsnip is more yang than a cabbage but less yang than brown rice. Remember that yin and yang are relative.

- A tomato is red which is a yang color but it has high water content, grows above the ground, and is considered a tropical fruit, which are all yin characteristics. We can then say that overall the tomato is yin.

- A carrot is dense, orange, grows downwards into the ground and has less water content; these characteristics are all yang. The part of the carrot that grows deepest in the soil is more yang, contracted, and usually thinner than the top. The top of the carrot is closer to the surface of the soil and changes to the green leafy part, which is the most yin. If you grab the carrot and eat it raw, the bottom might taste bitter while the top part is sweet. So even though the carrot is considered a yang vegetable, it has both expanding and contracting aspects. This is an example of how yin and yang are relative. The end of the carrot is relatively more yang than the top and greens.

If we look at vegetables, we can see that they all have a root, a connecting point, and leafy part. These different aspects of the vegetable become expanded depending on whether they are more yin or yang. When we eat vegetables, we can enjoy the similar energy.

- Root vegetables grow down into the ground and are more yang. In general we can say they are good for the lower part of the body and for helping us to feel grounded.

- Round vegetables have more balanced energy between yin and yang and give us energy in the center of the body, which helps us to feel steady and secure.

- Leafy vegetables grow up and out and nourish the upper body and head and help us to feel inspired, light, and youthful.

In cooking we can make dishes slightly more yin or yang through the use of fire (length of cooking and strength of heat), liquid, seasonings, and ingredients. For example, if we cook root vegetables in a stew for a long time, then the energy is contracting, downward, and strengthening (more yang). If we steam leafy vegetables quickly for a few minutes, the energy is expanding, upward, and refreshing (more yin).

We can make an incredible range of beautiful dishes that create balance around the center of the yin yang scale as you can see with the recipes in *Eat Me Now!*.

Yin and yang are simple tools that you can use to develop your intuition and artistic talent in the kitchen. Remember…that while it is great to look at yin and yang in daily eating and cooking, it is also important not to become fanatical about trying to balance the two energies. If you have fun and use a variety of ingredients and vary the cooking styles, you will naturally begin to create balance.

Exercise
See if you can figure out if you have more yin or yang characteristics by looking at the lists below.

Yang:
If you are, have or like:
- Sports
- Getting up early
- Movies
- The mountains
- Practical activities
- Outdoors
- Extravert
- Shorter
- Taking showers
- Shorter hair
- Socializing
- Salty foods
- Grains and stronger cooking

- Materially inclined
- Active

Yin:

If you are, have or like:
- Art
- Sleeping late
- TV
- The beach
- Thinking
- Indoors
- Introvert
- Taller
- Taking baths
- Longer hair
- Reading
- Sweet foods
- Vegetables and lighter cooking
- Spiritually inclined
- Gentle

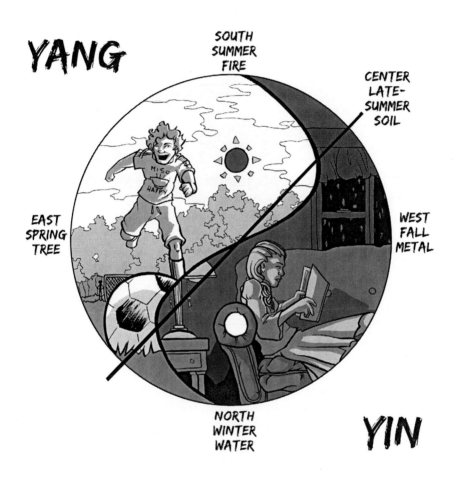

"The Yin and Yang of It All"

Five Elements

Different foods have different energies and everything is a unique interpretation of yin and yang. If we take a look at the seasons we can further understand the flow of energy from yin to yang and how foods make balance with the environment. We can also see why it makes sense to enjoy foods when they are in season.

In the summer, the atmosphere is extremely yang, hot, and active. To make balance, vegetation grows large, lush, and expanded, which is yin. Summer vegetables grow upward and outward like lettuces and leafy greens such as kale or collards. Some vegetables are more watery like tomatoes, watermelon, or cucumber while corn has lots of kernels on one cob. Fruit is plentiful, sweet, and juicy. When we eat these foods that grow upward or have more water content, then our energy moves upward and out, which helps to cool the body. This makes us to feel comfortable in the heat of summer.

In the winter, the atmosphere is extremely yin and still. To balance this yin, vegetation becomes contracted and quiet beneath the earth. Everything slows down. There aren't any vegetables growing so we use ones that have been harvested and stored in preparation for the cold weather. Produce that has been harvested is also dried such as beans, sea vegetables, fruits, and chestnuts. When we eat these foods, our energy moves downward and inward and we feel more grounded, stronger, and able to withstand the cold.

Spring and fall are transitional seasons. Spring is like gentle yang moving towards summer. Plants burst out of the ground such as scallions and leeks. Young grains like barley and wheat have this upward energy. Generally there is a feeling of excitement as new life begins after the stillness of winter. When we eat these foods we feel energized and uplifted.

In the fall, the extreme yang of summer begins its descent towards winter. The fall is like gentle yin as plants die back and leaves fall to the ground. Vegetables become more contracted and develop a round shape like cabbage, squash, and onions. Fruits such as melons and apples are abundant. There is desire to settle down after the activity of summer. These sweet foods center our energy and help us to feel calm and contented.

Late fall and early winter are becoming more yin and, in response, vegetables become contracted and grow beneath the earth like carrots, parsnips, and daikon. The greens are more contracted and stronger in taste. Rice is also a representation of late fall: compact and strengthening. These foods help our energy to become focused inside in preparation for the cold months ahead.

It is a good idea to use foods when they are in season, but also important to include something from the other seasons. This helps us to make a smooth transition from one season to the next. In the summer, we can remember winter with some stronger dishes using beans or sea vegetables. In the winter we can remember summer with lighter dishes using greens, leeks, or Chinese cabbage. The small yin is always present in the extreme yang and the small yang is always present in the extreme yin.

This is a very simplified introduction to the theory of the five stages of change, which was developed to further understand the flow between yin and yang. The ancient Chinese called the five elements fire (summer), soil (fall), metal (late fall), water (winter) and tree (spring). These naturally occurring forces were used to classify everything in the universe including the seasons, foods, direction, colors, tastes, and parts of the body.

Energy in Cooking

Cooking is a means whereby we actually change and transform the unique energy of food. The different ways that we prepare our food then helps our energy flow. Lighter cooking methods such as steaming or blanching move our energy upwards and out. Stir-frying creates active, lively, and quick energy. Pressure-cooking takes your energy deep inside and longer cooking methods like stews move your energy downwards. The ideal is to have a variety of cooking styles to encourage your energy to flow freely.

For example, in a meal you can choose to have one dish that is cooked for a long time and another that is cooked quickly. This would give you two different types of energy, one uplifting and light and the other strong and grounding.

You could also decide to make pressure cooked rice (very strengthening), a bean stew, (grounding and nourishing), and blanched greens and cauliflower, (light and uplifting). The energy of each dish combines to give you an overall feeling of balance.

Dishes that are cooked for 20 minutes or more are considered long-cooked whereas dishes that are ready in a few minutes are short-cooked. Dishes that are made with few ingredients create a more focused, clarifying effect and those that have many ingredients are more open and relaxing.

Examples of the Five Elements

- Fire
- Summer
- South
- Mid day
- Heart and small intestine
- Bitter taste
- Expanding energy
- Corn on the cob
- Leafy greens, lettuce, collards, kale
- Stir Fry

- Soil
- Late summer
- Center
- Mid afternoon
- Spleen, stomach pancreas
- Sweet taste
- Settled energy
- Round vegetables—cabbage, squash, onion, and turnips
- Melons
- Stews

- Metal
- Fall
- West
- Early evening
- Lung and large intestine
- Hot, pungent taste
- Condensed energy
- Root vegetables and strong greens—daikon and tops, carrot and tops, burdock
- Grains
- Pressure-cooking

- Water
- Winter
- North
- Night
- Kidney and bladder
- Salty taste
- Floating energy
- Sea Vegetables
- Beans
- Long sauté

- Tree
- Spring
- East
- Early morning
- Liver and gall bladder
- Uplifting energy
- Leeks, scallions, Chinese cabbage, celery, chives
- Lemons
- Sour taste
- Quick steaming

I have included the organs that relate to the different elements. The foods with the same element are nourishing to that organ. For example, light, uplifting cooking using leeks and Chinese cabbage with a dash of lemon would be cleansing to the liver. Steamed squash, onion, and cabbage are nourishing to the spleen, stomach and pancreas.

Enjoying the Power of Living Foods

Most of the foods in macrobiotics are living foods. Living foods include:
* whole grains
* dried beans
* vegetables
* fresh fruit
* seeds
* nuts
* fermented foods.

They are literally alive right up until you cook them.

Living foods are packed with energy and when combined with your unique energy create increased vitality and strength.

They also retain a high concentration of nutrients.

Processed foods, on the other hand, contain less nutrition and actually lose their nutritional value quickly.

For example, if you cut an apple in half, it quickly oxidizes and starts to turn brown. This spoiling occurs at different speeds with any food that is broken, cut or processed in some way.

"The Power of Living Foods"

Macrobiotics Is Eco-Friendly

Eating a macrobiotic diet means you will be taking positive steps towards the health of the planet and those who live in it.

Eating a grain and vegetable based diet:

- Saves lives and supports the rights of animals. 22 million animals are slaughtered on a daily basis in America alone.

- Reduces waste and air pollution. Eating an organic diet based around grains and vegetables makes the world a healthier place. Each year, the nation's factory farms, collectively produce two billion tons of manure, a substance that's rated by the Environmental Protection Agency (EPA) as one of the country's top 10 pollutants. The methane gas that is released by cows, pigs, and poultry is one of the highest contributions to global warming. There are also the ammonia gases from urine, poisonous gases that come off manure lagoons and toxic chemicals from pesticides that all contribute to unhealthy air.

- Protects water sources and reduces the pollution of waterways from fertilizers and manure. It takes 2,500 gallons of water to produce one pound of beef, but just 25 gallons of water to produce a pound of wheat.

- Reduces global hunger. 72 percent of all grain produced in the United States is fed to animals raised for slaughter. If the grain were given to people rather than animals, there would be enough food to feed the entire planet. In addition, animal agriculture drains the land of its natural life force including the destruction of the rain forests. The land is becoming depleted and over time will be unfit for food production. It takes at least twice as much land to raise and feed animals as it would to grow grains, beans, vegetables, and fruit for human consumption.

- Supports toxic- and chemical-free food. The EPA estimates that nearly 95 percent of pesticide residue in our diet comes from animal and dairy products. Meat and dairy products are also full of steroids and hormones.

- Lowers the chance of food-borne illnesses such as salmonella, e-coli and toxoplasmosis that are more readily found in chicken, beef, and pork.

Please note that I have included some fish recipes for those who want to make a slow transition away from animal food. Fish contains beneficial mono-unsaturated fats instead of the potentially more harmful saturated fats in meat. It is important to buy wild fish using sustainable methods of fishing (with a respect for the balance of the ocean), rather than farmed fish where there is no regard for the fish or the delicate ecosystem, and antibiotics are liberally used.

Say 'Yes!' to Organics

Organic foods are a fantastic way to enjoy ingredients in their pure and natural state.

Organic farming means to grow fruits, vegetables, and other plants without relying on synthetic pesticides, fungicides, herbicides, or fertilizers.

Organics are becoming much easier to find and even though they tend to be expensive they are worth it. The foods taste delicious and retain higher nutrition levels and flavor.

Organic food production reduces health risks because there is less exposure to chemicals and pesticides.

The farming methods help to protect our water sources and reduce toxic farming runoff and pollutants. Organic farmers work in harmony with nature and maintain a healthy ecosystem. Wildlife, natural hedges, wetlands, and other natural areas are protected and respected as a vital part of healthy farming.

In a world where we can't be sure how our foods are produced any more, choosing organics makes a huge difference to you and the health of the earth.

It is important to make the most of produce that can be grown in your area and climate. It is easier to feel comfortable in your environment if you enjoy the foods that are easily grown there.

Tasty Tip

Organic foods can be expensive. Roadside stands or farmers markets are great places to look for locally grown organic produce, which is often much cheaper. Try joining an organic food co-op where the prices are reduced and you can still buy smaller amounts of fresh produce.

Varying Vegetables
Instead of:-
Carrots use parsnips, squash
Onions use leeks, scallions
Squash use sweet potato
Cabbage use turnips, cauliflower
Watercress use kale, broccoli rabe, parsley
Kale use collards
Scallions use chives
Daikon use radishes, turnips
Cauliflower use broccoli

Getting Started

Macrobiotic Shopping List

The following list is for the ingredients that are required for the recipes in the book.

Whole Grains
- Short grain brown rice
- Medium grain brown rice
- Barley
- Millet
- Sweet corn

Cracked Grains
- Steel cut oats
- Oatmeal
- Cous cous
- Mochi
- Corn grits

Noodles
- Udon noodles
- Soba noodles
- Whole-grain pasta

Breads
- Sourdough grain wheat
- Spelt bread

- Whole-grain pita
- Whole-grain tortillas

Flours
- Whole wheat pastry flour
- Almond flour
- Oat flour

Vegetables
  Round or balanced energy:
- Cabbage, onions, squash, cauliflower, turnips, radishes
  Root or downward energy:
- Carrots, burdock, parsnips, daikon
  Leafy or upward energy:
- Chinese cabbage, watercress, broccoli, kale, collards, leeks, scallions, lettuce
  Vining or horizontal:
- Peas, cucumbers, summer squash, sweet potato, string beans, cucumber, snap peas

Beans
- Navy beans
- Lentils
- Chickpeas
- Kidney beans
- Pinto beans

Vegetable Protein
- Tofu
- Tempeh
- Seitan

Fish
- White Fish
- Tuna
- Salmon
- Organic frozen fish sticks
- Organic frozen cod fillets

Seeds and Nuts
- Sesame
- Pumpkin
- Sunflower
- Almonds
- Walnuts
- Peanuts

Sea Vegetables
- Nori
- Arame
- Kombu
- Wakame
- Hiziki
- Dulse
- Agar Agar

Oils
- Sesame
- Olive
- Safflower

Condiments and Seasonings
- Shoyu
- Brown rice or barley miso
- Brown rice vinegar
- Umeboshi vinegar
- Tahini or toasted sesame butter
- Peanut butter (creamy)
- Umeboshi plums
- Sauerkruat
- Dill pickles
- Shiso powder

Beverages
- Kukicha
- Apple or other sugar free Juice
- Amasake
- Various herbal teas
- Green tea
- Rice, oat or almond milk
- Carrot juice

Sweeteners
- Barley malt
- Rice syrup
- Maple syrup
- Jelly (no added sugar)

Fruits
- Apples, pears
- Berries—raspberries, strawberries, blueberries.
- Grapes
- Lemon
- Oranges/ tangerines

Snacks
- Puffed cereal
- Rice cakes, corn cakes
- Raisins
- Granola
- Cookies (no added sugar)
- Popcorn
- Apple sauce
- Canned fruit (no added sugar)
- Dried fruit like apricots and apples

Instant Foods
- Miso soup
- Miso ramen

- Noodles in a bowl
- Rice in a bowl
- Packaged brown rice
- Packaged cous cous
- Soy cheese pizza pockets
- Veggie burgers
- Waffles
- Ravioli
- Organic tomato sauce
- Pesto sauce

Utensils:
- Stainless pressure cooker
- Various stainless steel pots with lids
- Cast Iron Skillet with lid
- Suribachi (mortar)
- Surikoji (pestle)
- Wooden spoons
- Wooden cutting board
- Blender
- Sushi mat (bamboo mat for covering food and making sushi)
- Vegetable cutting knife
- Can opener (for college)
- Hot water bottle (not for cooking but very useful)

There is a comprehensive list of snack foods in the Eating Well in College section.

Please use Organic foods and produce whenever possible.

Getting Set Up:

Cooking does take time but the benefits are awesome: stronger health, more vitality, and an overall sense of wellbeing. Enjoying home-cooked meals is the most powerful way to nourish the self.

Look through the recipes in *Eat Me Now!* and use the shopping list before going to the supermarket or health food store.

Make sure you have all the ingredients to make the recipe.

Buy organic foods whenever possible; next choose, locally grown; and if all else fails, supplement from the supermarket to keep the variety going.

Keep foods in stock that can be used in a pinch such as pasta, brown rice, sea salt, shoyu, miso, cans of beans, nut butters, jam (no added sugar), instant natural foods like miso ramen, instant miso soup, boxed brown rice or cous cous, and rice cakes.

Keep some basic ingredients to liven up simple dishes; olive oil, brown rice vinegar, ginger, hot sesame oil, garlic, lemon, cumin, umeboshi vinegar, dried herbs such as parsley or basil, organic tomato sauce, hummus, jars of pesto, black pepper.

Keep a spare loaf of sourdough bread in the freezer.

Raid Mom's pantry when you come home from college to stock up on items to take back.

Store your dried foods in glass jars; even label them if you aren't sure of the ingredients. They are easier to find and create more order in the kitchen.

Some useful utensils are: a hand-held blender, pepper mill, a few stainless steel pots, wooden cutting board, vegetable cutting knife, wooden spoons. A cast iron skillet is very handy for many dishes. Wooden utensils have a more gentle effect on the food.

A vegetable skimmer is a great tool for taking vegetables out of boiling water; it is inexpensive and can be found at most cookware stores.

A Note on Cookware

The ideal cookware is stainless steel, cast iron or enamel; they last longer, are toxin free and help to cook ingredients more efficiently and easily.

A small metal steamer is another great utensil for the kitchen; you can use it to reheat leftovers, steam vegetables and tofu, or refresh bread.

Pressure Cookers

Modern pressure cookers are very safe and easy to use and are quite different than their ancestors, which tended to scare people. Today's pressure cookers have at least three valves for safety and will automatically release pressure should it build too high.

This is a great method for cooking grains and beans. It cuts down on cooking time and because less liquid is lost, more vitamins and minerals are retained than with conventional cooking methods.

Fun in the Kitchen

The first step is to get in the kitchen and have a go at making one new dish.

Have a blast cooking. Happy, lively energy makes for tasty, energized food. Listen to music, chat with friends, or get them to join in with the meal preparation.

If you are new to cooking, begin with the easier recipes first.

Prepare well. This cuts way down on the cooking time. Read the recipe through before beginning to cook. Collect all the ingredients you are going to need for the recipe. Cut all the vegetables first before you begin to cook.

Vary the use of the flame. It is often seems faster to cook everything on a high flame but this often creates intense, un-relaxed cooking. Use a medium flame to bring water, rice, or beans to a boil and then turn the flame down. Long stews can be cooked on a low flame. Stir fries can use a high flame. Low heat has a calming effect and creates steady, strong energy. High heat cooking is more intense, yet bright and energetic.

Keep things tasty. Try not to make the same things over and over. Change an ingredient here, a vegetable there, or create a new dressing to spice up your meals. The recipes are simply guidelines so feel free to create new variations of your own.

Clean up as you go along. Wash up any pans, wipe down the cutting board and knife between each vegetable, wipe down the counters, and put away extra ingredients or vegetables. Hang dishtowels to dry after use.

You can cut vegetables in different ways to make your meals more interesting. When you cut carrots on an angle, then you are making balance between the top and bottom of the carrot. It also makes them taste sweeter. You can cut other vegetables on an angle such as scallions, celery, daikon, parsnips, leeks or leafy greens. If you want to make matchsticks, you cut small sticks across each of the angled slices.

For round vegetables like radishes or onions, you can cut them in half between the root and greens. Then lie the flat side down and cut across between the root and greens so that each piece is still a part of the whole. These pieces are known as half moons

Tasty Tip

Remember that creating and cooking your meals is empowering and puts you in charge of your health and well-being.

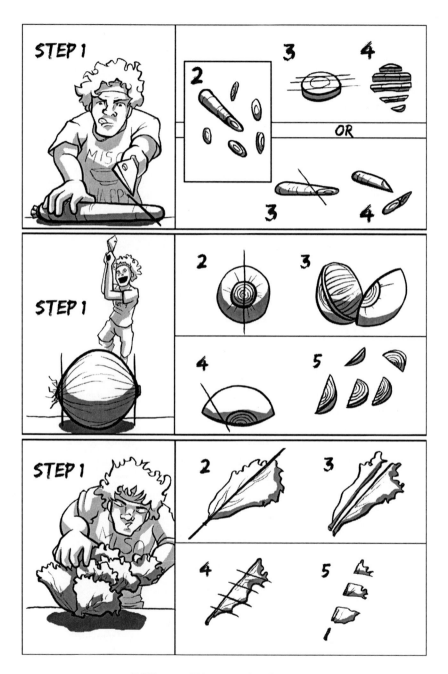

Different Ways to Cut Veggies

Tasty Tips

Make extra amounts of rice, beans, or longer cooked vegetable dishes. They can be enjoyed the next day or made into a new dish such as a soup, sushi, or re-fried.

Serve dressings on the side so lighter cooked vegetables stay fresh and can be used again.

Make enough breakfast cereals for at least 2 days. They can be quickly reheated which will save time in the morning.

Try and have some freshly cooked vegetables everyday.

"Dining is and always was a great artistic opportunity."
—Frank Lloyd Wright

Weird and Wonderful Foods

You may not of heard of some of these foods, but they are a great addition to your diet and worth experimenting with. Many have a powerful healing effect and can be used to add energy and creativity to your cooking. Most of these items can be purchased in natural food stores and also in supermarkets.

Whole Grains - are grains in their unprocessed, living form. These include brown rice, hulled whole barley, millet, whole oats, wheat berries, spelt, whole rye and corn on the cob.

Miso - a thick paste made from soybeans and contains living enzymes; miso is complete nutrition; it is strengthening and an antioxidant. It is good for overall health and gives you lots of energy as well as beautiful skin and hair. There are many different types of miso. Barley and brown rice are most commonly used and white miso makes great sauces and dressings.

Kuzu - a white powder that is extracted from the center of the wild and invasive kuzu root. Kuzu is strengthening, balancing, good for the digestion and immune system, and for relaxing tense muscles.

Umeboshi Plums - extremely salty sour plums that are an antioxidant and good for longevity, stamina, digestion, circulation, and preventing fatigue. Umeboshi helps to maintain an alkaline blood balance. Umeboshi can also be purchased as a vinegar or in paste form.

Agar Agar Flakes - the vegan gelatin and comes from a sea vegetable. Agar agar helps to relax the digestion, is calming and cooling. It is often used to make a fruit aspic known as kanten.

Shoyu - a liquid made from soybeans, sea salt and wheat, which is naturally fermented. Good for circulation, the heart, and balances acid/alkaline in blood, adds amino acids, and stimulates appetite.

Tofu - is a soybean product made from cooked and crushed beans. It is very high in protein, calcium and vitamins. It actually contains 23 percent more calcium by weight than dairy milk. Tofu is a great diet food because it is highly nutritious yet low in calories.
It is an extremely versatile food and can be prepared in a few minutes. Tofu can be baked, fried, boiled, steamed, mashed, blended, added to a variety of vegetable dishes, or used in soups.

Sea Salt - is salt in its natural form, which means it still contains trace minerals. Natural sea salt helps to create our blood and body fluids, which also contain sodium chloride and many varieties of minerals. Dishes prepared with sea salt have a better taste and nutritional value then those with refined salt. Refined salt has high levels of sodium chloride and drying agents added which make it very difficult for the body to assimilate and utilize.

Burdock - is a wild vegetable that grows almost everywhere in America. The part of the burdock that is edible is the root and the young fresh greens. Burdock is long, thin, and brown in color; resembling a stick. It is high in B vitamins and is very good for increasing strength and vitality.

Barley malt - is a thick, dark, slow-digesting sweetener made from sprouted barley. It has a malt-like flavor. Malted barley has a high complement of enzymes for converting its starch supply into simple sugars; it also contains protein, which is needed for yeast nutrition. Barley malt helps to relax the digestion and can be used to sweeten tea, cereals, and desserts.

Brown rice syrup - is a naturally processed sweetener, made from sprouted brown rice. It is thick and mild-flavored and about one half as sweet as sugar. Brown rice syrup is a healthful, tasty alternative and can be used to on bread and to sweeten cereals, drinks, and desserts.

Shiso Powder - this is a great condiment to sprinkle on grains or vegetable dishes. Shiso is rich in chlorophyll, calcium and iron. It also contains linoleic acid, which helps to dissolve cholesterol

Sea Vegetables - sea vegetables act as filters in the sea and filter wonderful ocean minerals that cannot be found in land food. When we eat sea vegetables they help to cleanse our blood, and smoothly discharge toxins and excess fat, as well as providing important nutrition. There are many varieties each with a unique color and flavor. Sea vegetables can be used in soups, bean dishes, and sautéed with vegetables, or added to salads.

Eating Well at College

Eating healthy food at college can appear daunting at first. However, with a little planning you can create nutritious, energy-giving meals and snacks that will help to keep you energized and mentally alert.

Healthy Choices

Instead of:
- Fried foods
- Refined grains (like white bread and white rice, refined pasta)
- Milk
- French fries
- Sweetened drinks and sodas
- Sweetened desserts (like cookies, cake, or ice cream)

Go for:
- Grilled dishes
- Whole grains (like whole wheat bread, cous cous, oatmeal, brown rice and whole wheat pasta)
- Rice, oat or almond milk
- Baked potato, cooked veggies or salad
- Water, herbal teas or sugar free juice and spritzers
- Fruit, sugar free jelly, applesauce, maple sweetened cookies, roasted nuts and raisins or dried apricots.

Keep your room stocked with healthy snacks and foods you can grab when you're hungry:
- Granola bars
- Oatmeal (packets)
- Instant brown rice
- Instant cous cous
- Miso ramen noodles
- Sugar free boxed cereals
- Packaged miso soup
- Pre popped natural popcorn
- Rice cakes, corn thins, crackers, pita bread
- Trail mix
- Roasted nuts
- Toasted seeds
- Jars of pesto
- Cans of tuna
- Shoyu
- Sea salt
- Sesame and olive oil
- Brown rice vinegar
- Umeboshi plums
- Peanut or almond butter
- Sugar free canned fruit
- Sugar free cookies
- Boxed sugar free juices
- Spritzers (no sugar added)
- Small containers of apple sauce
- Rice syrup
- Kukicha and green tea bags
- Herbal tea bags

If you have a fridge:
- Rice or almond milk
- Soy yogurt
- Baby carrots

- Hummus
- Fresh fruit
- Spring water
- Carrot juice
- Dill pickles
- Sauerkraut
- Whole wheat or spelt sourdough bread
- Jelly (no sugar added)
- Pure maple syrup
- Cucumbers
- Lemon

Healthy Eating Tips

Regular Meals

Eating 3 meals at the same time each day will give you lasting energy and keep your metabolism active. Pack healthy snacks such as fruit or a granola bar when you are busy or have to miss a meal for a class.

Food provides energy on all levels and is essential for your brain and thinking. Skipping meals can cause low blood sugar, feeling drowsy in class, trouble concentrating, feeling down, or headaches.

Whole Living Foods

Eating healthy whole food meals will help to ensure that you get all the nutrition you need to stay healthy! Be sure to eat different combinations of grains, beans, nuts, seeds, fruits, and vegetables throughout the day. Eat about 40% whole grains and grain products; 20% protein including beans, nuts, seeds, tofu, tempeh, seitan, or fish; 40% vegetables including sea vegetables and fruits.

Drinking Water

Drinking water is important both internally for your organs and system and externally for providing natural moisture to your skin and giving you a fresh glow. Remember, that eating a vegetable-based diet naturally increases your intake of fluids so you don't need as much water as someone on a SAD

(Standard American Diet). Too much water can flush out important minerals and make you feel weak and drained.

On the other hand, waiting until you are thirsty to drink often means you are already partially dehydrated. If you tend to go for long periods without drinking anything, try to have some water even if you are not really thirsty. If the idea of drinking water isn't appealing, add a squeeze of lemon or orange or a drop of peppermint essential oil to make it a refreshing treat. You can also enjoy herbal teas and vegetable-based drinks.

Dining in Restaurants

The portions in restaurants are often more than one serving size and they're getting bigger. When dining out, plan on taking half of your meal home or spilt it with a friend and save on both your health and your purse. When eating at the dining hall, take a small portion at first. You can always go back for more if you are still hungry.

Choose Italian, Chinese, Greek, Japanese, seafood or salad bar restaurants as they all have healthy options from which to choose.

Variety is the Key to a Healthy Macrobiotic Diet

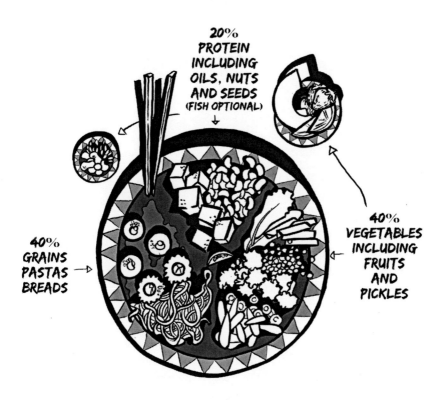

**20%
PROTEIN
INCLUDING
OILS, NUTS
AND SEEDS
(FISH OPTIONAL)**

**40%
GRAINS
PASTAS
BREADS**

**40%
VEGETABLES
INCLUDING
FRUITS
AND
PICKLES**

"The Macro Food Plate"

Bare Necessities

Menu:

- **Basic Brown Rice Recipe**
- **Basic Noodles**
- **Basic Broth**
- **Basic Pasta**
- **Simple Miso Soup**
- **Sourdough Bread**
- **Re-Freshening Bread**
- **Roasting Nuts**
- **Toasting Seeds**
- **Simple Blanched Vegetables**
- **Simple Steamed Vegetables**

These recipes are the foundational ones to get you started. They are the basics and can be jazzed up with extra dressings, sauces and ingredients. The additional recipes throughout the book will help you to do just that.

If you are new to cooking, don't panic!! The basic recipes are very easy to prepare.

I suggest you begin to include them on a daily basis.

Practice with the brown rice recipe, one of the vegetable recipes and then toast up some nuts or seeds. Voila. You have the beginnings of a great, energy giving meal.

By simply including these dishes into your diet, you are leaping into a healthy and lively lifestyle.

Remember that cooking is a creative art, relying, to a great extent, on your unique energy and intuition. Seasoning can make or break the flavor of a dish.

Although I specify how much to use in the recipes, sometimes a little more or a little less is needed depending on your needs, taste, and preference. It is always safer to use a light hand when seasoning because you can add more. Don't worry if a dish doesn't turn out exactly how you imagined the first time around. Practice does make perfect and small adjustments such as a little less water or a little more oil can make all the difference.

Brown Rice Is More Than Just Nice

Brown rice is a very versatile grain and can be used in many dishes such as soups, stir-fries, stews and dessert.

Brown rice has a complete balance of protein, healthy carbohydrates and minerals and can be eaten on a daily basis. It helps to strengthen the digestion, blood and immune system. Brown rice improves concentration, which is perfect for studying and schoolwork. It also makes us feel focused, calm, and develops strength and stamina.

Cooking Tips:

Why pressure cook rice?
- Cooks the rice from inside out.
- Makes it possible for to assimilate and digest all the nutritional elements.
- Brings out the naturally sweet taste in rice and so the flavor is more delicious.
- Helps accelerate physical, mental and spiritual development.
- Provides added strength and vitality.

*If you don't have a pressure cooker, no worries. You can boil your rice in a heavy pot with a lid and it will still be great for your health.

Reasons to soak rice before cooking.
- Helps to lighten up and open each grain.
- Aids in the thorough assimilation and digestion of all the nutrients.
- Has a deeply relaxing effect on the body.
- Brings out the full flavor of the rice.

You can soak your rice before going to school or work in the morning and then cook it when you get home in the evening.

Make sure you soak the rice in the water that is used for cooking. Do not discard the soaking water and then add more water because the rice will turn out soggy.

Your rice will turn out better if you cook 2 cups. You will also have some leftover to use over the next few days.

Leftover rice can be re-steamed in a steamer, fried on its own or with vegetables and seasoned with a little shoyu, rolled in sushi, made into rice balls or added to soup.

Tasty Tips

Don't waste! When serving food, try not to pile up your plate. Only take what you can comfortably eat. You can always go back for seconds.

Basic Brown Rice Recipe

S V ST C

Serves: 4-6 people

Preparation and cooking time:
at least 3 hours soaking before cooking. 40-45 minutes cooking

Ingredients:
2 cups medium grain brown rice rinsed (short, long or basmati brown rice can be used instead)
2 1/2 cups spring water
1/4 teaspoon sea salt
If you want to cut back on salt use 1 inch strip rinsed kombu instead

Utensils:
Pressure cooker or heavy pot with a lid, flame deflector

Preparations:
Place the rinsed rice and water in a pressure cooker and soak for three to five hours.

Add the salt or kombu and cover with a lid.

Place the pressure cooker on a medium flame and bring up to pressure. When the pressure is up reduce flame to medium/low. Place a flame defector under the pressure cooker. Cook for about 35-40 minutes.

When the rice is cooked, remove the pressure cooker from the heat and allow pressure to come down naturally.

Remove the rice from pot with a damp wooden spoon or rice paddle. Take the rice out in sections going around the pot.

Place the rice in a large wooden or ceramic bowl and gently separate the grains with the rice paddle.

Cover the rice with a sushi mat until you are ready to serve.

Boiling Method
Place the rinsed rice and water in a heavy pot and soak for three to five hours.

Add the salt or kombu and cover with a lid.

Place the pot on a medium flame and bring to a boil. Reduce the flame to medium/low. Place a flame defector under the pot. Cook for about 40-45 minutes.

Remove the pan from the heat.

Remove the rice from pot with a damp wooden spoon or rice paddle. Take the rice out in sections going around the pot.

Place the rice in a large wooden or ceramic bowl and gently separate the grains with the rice paddle.

Cover the rice with a sushi mat and serve.

If you don't have a lid for your pot use a plate about the same size or slightly larger than the top of the pot. Place the plate in a dish towel, bring up the sides and tie around the top of the plate. Use the knot as your pot handle and place on top of the pot.

> **"Rice is great if you're really hungry**
> **and want to eat two thousand of something."**
> **—Mitch Hedberg**

Noodles and Pasta

Here are some easy tips for cooking great noodles and pasta. Noodles refers to all varieties from all origins, whereas pasta refers specifically to Italian style noodle products

Udon is a Japanese noodle made from wheat flour and salt. They are relaxing and de-stressing.

Soba is a Japanese noodle made from buckwheat flour, wheat flour and salt. They are strengthening and stamina building.

Pasta is made from wheat flour without salt and are nourishing and calming.

Hints for cooking great noodles and pasta

Use a large pot with lots of water at a full boil.

Season the water with salt.

(Oil isn't necessary and doesn't prevent the pasta from sticking).

To prevent the noodles from sticking, use plenty of water, keep the water at a full boil, stir well, especially at the beginning, and don't overcrowd the pot with too much pasta.

You can cook the pasta until it is almost done and then finish it in your sauce or broth.

If your sauce is a little too thick or too dry, add some of the pasta water.

Match the pasta to the sauce based on the solidity of the pasta and the thickness of the sauce. Generally speaking, heartier sauces go with sturdier pastas and thinner pasta with brothy sauces.

It isn't necessary to rinse your pasta unless you're making a cold pasta preparation like pasta salad. Rinsing the pasta reduces the surface starch and thus prevents the sauce from clinging to it.

Japanese noodles can be rinsed in cold water to maintain their texture and flavor.

The basic serving size is 4 ounces of dried although it does vary very slightly according to the shape of the pasta.

Basic Noodles

S V R

Serves: 4 people

Preparation and cooking time: 15 minutes

Ingredients:

1 packet noodles (soba or udon)
6 cups spring water

Utensils:

Medium pot, strainer

Preparation:

Place the water in a pot and bring to a boil on a medium flame.
Add the noodles and fan them around the pot to prevent sticking.
Stir well and cook at a slow boil for about 10 minutes or until tender.
Place the noodles in a strainer and rinse well under cold water.

Note:

To make sure the noodles are cooked, remove one noodle from the pot and break one end. If the outside and inside are the same color, the noodles are ready.

Or you can try throwing a noodle at the wall. If it sticks it's done!

Soba noodles take less time to cook than udon. Thinner noodles cook faster than thick noodles.

Basic Pasta

S V R

Serves: 4 people

Preparation and cooking time: 15 minutes

Ingredients:

1 packet pasta
10 cups spring water
1 teaspoon sea salt

Utensils:

Large pot, strainer, wooden spoon

Preparation:

Place the water in a pot and bring to a boil on a medium flame.
Add the pasta and fan them around the pot to prevent sticking.
Stir well and cook at a slow boil for about 10 minutes or until tender.
Drain the pasta in a strainer and add to any prepared sauce.

Basic Stock

S V R

Serves: 4 people

Preparation and cooking time: 5 minutes

Ingredients:

1 inch piece kombu rinsed
4 cups spring water
1/4 teaspoon sea salt

Utensils:

Medium pot

Preparation:

Place the water and kombu in a pot and bring to a boil on a medium flame.
Remove the kombu and save it for later soups.
Add the sea salt and simmer for 1 minute.
This broth is ready as a basic stock for
Any other soups such as bean, shoyu or miso.

For a quick broth for noodles, add 1-2 tablespoons of shoyu to the broth and simmer on a low flame for 3 minutes. Serve with chopped scallions and fresh ginger.

Leftover pieces of vegetables can be added to this stock such as onion skins, carrot tops and corn cobs. Remove when the water boils and before seasoning with shoyu.

Simple Miso Soup

S V ST C E

This is a basic recipe for miso soup. Feel free to add different vegetables such as cabbage, leek, carrots, corn or daikon.

Serves: 4 people

Preparation and cooking time: 10-15 minutes

Ingredients

1 small onion sliced
1 teaspoon wakame flakes
1/2 cup tofu diced
4 cups spring water
1 leaf of kale finely sliced
1 scallion finely sliced
1 generous tablespoon brown rice or barley miso diluted in a little water
Pinch of fresh ginger (optional)

Utensils:

Medium pan with lid

Preparation:

Place the onions in a pan and cover with water.
Bring to a boil and simmer for 3 minutes.
Add the rest of the water, cover and bring to a boil.
Add the wakame and tofu.
Continue to simmer for another 5 minutes.
Season with the diluted miso and turn the flame to very low.
Add the kale and cook for 3 minutes.
Serve garnished with scallions and ginger.

Sourdough Bread

Sourdough breads are made without yeast and instead use a natural process of fermentation of grains or starters to make the dough rise.

Yeasted bread can cause the stomach to bloat, weaken the intestines, thin the blood, and create mucus, especially in the sinuses.

There are many different types of sourdough bread including whole-wheat, rice, spelt, kamut, mixed grain, rye and other lighter varieties consisting of combined flours.

It is now possible to find sourdough bread in many supermarkets.

Re-Freshening Bread

S V R

When you steam bread, it makes it much softer and easier to digest. It has a relaxing effect on the nervous system and doesn't create hardness or mucus in the body.

When bread gets hard or dried out, re-freshening can make it taste as if it has been freshly baked. Steamed bread has a moist texture and the flavor is brought out so that it tastes wonderful.

Serves: 1 person

Preparation and cooking time: 5 minutes

Ingredients:
2 slices sourdough bread
1/2 cup water

Utensils:
Medium pot with lid, steamer

Preparation:
Place the water in a pot and bring to boil on a medium flame.
Place the bread in the steamer and steam covered for five minutes.
Serve with the variety of spreads from *Between the Slices*.
Peanut butter and jelly taste awesome on refreshed bread. Try peanut butter or almond butter with rice syrup for a scrumptious alternative.

Tasty Tips

When cutting vegetables or fruits, remember to wipe your cutting board and knife. This helps to keep the flavors distinct and the kitchen organized.

Nuts are one of the best plant sources of protein.

They are rich in fiber, phytonutrients (which strengthen immune function) and antioxidants such as Vitamin E and selenium.

Nuts are also high in monounsaturated and polyunsaturated fats (omega 3—the good fats), which have all been shown to lower LDL cholesterol.
Nuts are so full of nutrients that they quell hunger pangs with fewer calories compared with other snack foods that often provide lots of calories with minimal nutrition.

The best nuts for daily use are almonds, walnuts, peanuts, hazelnuts and pecans.

Roasting Nuts

S V R

Ingredients:
2 cups of nuts
Only use only one kind of nut on a baking sheet.
Different nuts can be roasted together by using more than one baking sheet.

Utensils:
Baking sheet, bowl, storage container

Preparation:
Pre-heat the oven at 300 degrees.
Place the nuts on a baking sheet.
Bake in the oven for 10 minutes.
Remove and place in a bowl to cool.
Store in a glass airtight jar.
Enjoy as a snack or chop and serve over grains and vegetables.

Simple Snack

Walnuts and raisins are a healthy way to satisfy chocolate cravings. Mix 1/2 cup of each and enjoy as a nutritious snack.

The Sizzling Seeds of Change

Seeds contain all the nutrients needed to nourish the growth of a new plant so their high nutrient content isn't a surprise.

Under the right conditions, seeds can lay dormant for thousands of years and yet still be able to sprout and produce a plant. This shows that they are full of living energy.

Seeds are an excellent source of healthy minerals, niacin and folic-acid. They are among the best plant sources of iron and zinc.

One ounce of pumpkin seeds contains almost twice as much iron as three ounces of skinless chicken breast.

Seeds are high in fiber and are a great source of protein.

Sesame seeds are extremely high in the bone-building mineral calcium, which is great news for anyone who has trouble tolerating dairy products.

Seeds are a rich source of vitamin E and omega 3 fatty acids.

"To see things in the seed, that is genius."
—Lao Tzu

Toasting Seeds

SVR

Ingredients:
2 cups of seeds rinsed and strained
(Sesame seeds are so tiny that other objects can easily get mixed in. It is a good idea to place them on a plate and quickly sort through to remove any little stones or twigs.)

Utensils:
Large Skillet. Wooden spoon

Preparation:
Warm the skillet on a medium flame and add the seeds.

Dry roast on a high flame for about 3-5 minutes. Move the seeds back and forth continuously with a wooden spoon. If they start to pop and jump rapidly, turn the flame down to low.

To check if the sesame seeds are toasted, dip a dry stainless steel teaspoon into the seeds. If the seeds stick to the spoon they need more toasting. If the spoon comes away clean, they are ready.

Remove and place the seeds in a bowl to cool.

Store in an airtight glass jar.

Enjoy as a snack or sprinkle over grains and vegetables.

Another Quick Snack

Nuts, seeds and dried fruit make a wonderful snack that gives you lots of vitality and nourishment. Combine 1/4 cup of any seeds, nuts, chopped dried apricots or apples and raisins. Add a pinch of sea salt. Place in a paper bag, shake well and relish. Great for get-togethers and parties.

**"No man in the world has more courage than the man
who can stop after eating one peanut."
—Channing Pollock**

Veg Out

Blanching is a very easy way to cook vegetables. This method of quickly cooking vegetables in boiling water keeps them bright, refreshing and crispy, brings the vitamins out to the surface and provides light, uplifting, positive type energy.

Many different types of vegetables can be blanched. Just remember to cut them in small pieces so they can cook quickly.

City living has a drying effect on the body, as there isn't much natural green around. Eating blanched vegetables on a daily basis gives us some of the freshness we are missing from nature.

Simple Blanched Vegetables

SVRCE

The vegetables can be blanched in the same water. This dish is most beneficial when it is made fresh every day.

Serves: 2

Preparation and cooking time: 7 minutes

Ingredients:
1 carrot rinsed and finely sliced
1 cup Chinese cabbage rinsed and finely sliced
1 cup string beans rinsed and sliced in half

Utensils:
Medium pan with lid, cutting board, knife, serving bowl

Preparation:
Place the water in a pan.
Cover with a lid and bring to a boil on a medium flame.
When the water is boiling, turn the flame to high.
Drop the carrots into the water. After a few seconds remove the carrots with a slotted spoon or a strainer. Place in a serving bowl.
Wait for the water to come back to a boil. Add the Chinese cabbage and cook for about 1 minute. Remove and add to the carrots.
Wait for the water to come back to a boil. Add the string beans and cook for about 1 minute. Remove and add to the other vegetables.
Mix gently and pour off any extra water.
Serve.

You can choose from lots of different vegetables and blanch only one or many.
Examples of veggies are cauliflower, broccoli, cabbage, summer squash, leeks, kale, collards, watercress, peas, and corn.
Blanch the vegetable, which has the sweetest or mildest flavor first.

Blanch those with a strong flavor such as celery, greens or radishes last.

Blanched vegetables taste tremendous with the creamy tofu dressing in the *Vital Veggies* section.

When washing vegetables, fill your sink or a bowl with water and submerge them. This saves water and makes it easy to thoroughly clean the produce. Afterwards, use the water for your plants.

Veg In

The steaming method of cooking helps to bring out the naturally sweet taste in vegetables, which makes us feel relaxed and nourished. When you steam vegetables until they are very soft, your energy stays deep inside and creates warmth. Whole cooked vegetables give you a feeling of completeness. Steaming is good for vitality, stamina and provides enduring energy. If you want a lighter effect, then the vegetables can be steamed for a shorter time.

Simple Steamed Vegetables

S V ST C

Servings: 2 people

Preparation and cooking time: 25 minutes

Ingredients:
1 small carrot rinsed
1 small turnip rinsed with a cross cut into the stem part
3 brussel sprouts rinsed with a cross cut into the stem part
Pinch sea salt
1/2 cup spring water

Utensils:
Medium pot with lid, stainless steel or bamboo steamer

Preparation:
Place the water in a pan.
Place the steamer in the pan
Place the carrot, turnip and brussel sprouts in the steamer.
Add a pinch of sea salt.
Cover with a lid and bring to a boil on a high flame.
Turn the flame to low and simmer for 15-20 minutes.
Remove from heat and place in a serving bowl.

Different vegetables can be used such as onions, winter squash, leek, cabbage, parsnips, or daikon.

Buying Greens

Fresh greens have a deep color and smell very fresh with no dry, yellowing or wilted leaves. Make sure the stems are moist and not brown or dry. If the bunch feels heavy with tight, firm and full leaves then they are newly picked. Greens are almost all water so if they feel light, they are drying out. When washing leeks, slice them in half lengthwise so you can clean the inner part.

Extras to add to your meals:

You can use toasted nori on a daily basis. This tasty mineral rich sea vegetable is already prepared and can be used in soup, on top of rice or as a quick snack.

Include pickles such as dill, sauerkraut, kimchee or even a little umeboshi plum. They are great for digestion and provide valuable enzymes.

To jazz up your rice, make a dressing or sauce to go on top. Check out the dressing ideas in Vital Veggies.

An exercise to Start using brown rice in your meals.

Monday: Make the basic brown rice recipe.
Tuesday: Make a recipe that uses leftover brown rice from the grains section.
Wednesday: Use the leftover grain dish in a soup recipe.
Thursday through Saturday: Repeat the above steps.
Sunday: Make a new recipe from the grains section.

An exercise to start using vegetables in your meals.

Monday: Make the blanched vegetables.
Tuesday: Make the steamed vegetables.
Wednesday: Make the blanched vegetables and add a dressing from the vegetable section.
Thursday: Make enough steamed vegetables for dinner and to save for lunch on Friday.
Friday: Make the blanched vegetables with another dressing for dinner.
Saturday: Make the steamed vegetables and include the cool cucumbers from the Vital Veggies section.
Sunday: Make the blanched vegetables and the lightly sautéed Chinese cabbage and wakame from the Vital Veggies section.

You can then combine the grain and vegetable exercise together.

> "Continuous effort—not strength or intelligence—
> is the key to unlocking our potential."
> —Sir Winston Churchill
> 1874-1965, Former British Prime Minister

Tasty Tips

Make a travel bag that you can have ready for car rides or trips. Fill it with healthy snacks, a natural salad dressing, rice cakes, toasted nuts and seeds, dried fruit, umeboshi, instant miso soup, tea bags and boxed juice

Brilliant Breakfasts

- Breakfast is the meal that follows a night of fasting.
- The first meal of the day needs to be gentle on the digestion yet nutritious enough to get your energy moving.
- Breakfast is eaten when the sun is in the east, which provides the positive, upward energy of the morning.
- Morning energy is perfect for moving out of the home and going to school or work.
- Your breakfast should be light and uplifting to compliment this rising energy.
- A large overly sweet or rich meal will make you feel lethargic, sleepy and unmotivated, better suited to Sundays and when on vacation.

Reasons to Eat Breakfast

Just like our cars, it is important to put healthy gas in our fuel tank otherwise we may feel like we're running on empty all day.

A high-fiber, low-fat, low sugar breakfast promotes healthy weight control and energy rather than the "refined" breakfasts most people are eating today.

'Refined' means; donuts, enriched cereals with sugar, white flour pancakes and muffins, white bread, bagels and morning cakes.

Breakfast doesn't have to be fancy to meet nutritional needs and you can get started on simple, easy and healthful breakfasts.

Skipping breakfast doesn't help to maintain a healthy weight or stay thin. Most people who skip breakfast tend to eat more calories throughout the day.

More Convincing Reasons

Kids who don't eat breakfast have less energy for learning in school and feel more tired towards the end of the day.

There is a tendency towards a higher body mass index (BMI), which is a sign of being overweight.

Eating breakfast helps kids do better in school especially when it comes to mental clarity and focus.

Breakfast provides the vitality to participate in physical activities, maintain energy levels and develop healthy eating habits throughout the day.

What Should You Eat?

Whole grains cooked into hot cereals because they provide balanced nutrition, give warmth and stamina and are gentle on the digestion.

They keep the blood sugar balanced, stabilize the emotions and improve concentration.

Breakfast is not meant to be a dessert. Foods can be mildly sweet but too much will affect blood sugar, create an acid condition and make you sleepy throughout the day.

General Ideas:

Breakfast can be simple but it can also be varied.

- Whole grains:—hot cereals, breads, sugar free muffins, sugar free cereals, whole grain pancakes, noodles.
- Protein such as tofu, hummus, nuts or seeds
- Vegetables and fruits
- Herbal teas, fruit juice, smoothies
- Vegetable or miso soups

If you find yourself skipping breakfast because you're too rushed, try these quick breakfasts. They're easy to grab on the way out the door or can be prepared the night before:

- Baggie of whole-grain, sugar-free cereal (can mix with fresh berries)
- Hummus on a rice cake or corn thins
- Fresh fruit
- Whole-grain muffin
- Granola bar
- Dried fruit
- Whole grain toaster waffles
- Steamed bread spread with peanut butter and jelly
- Steamed bread with peanut butter and sauerkraut
- Cold oatmeal cooked the night before
- Soy yoghurt
- Sugar free granola with oat or rice milk.

"Brilliant Breakfasts"

Menu:

- **Hot Cereals**
- **Basic Oatmeal**
- **Softly Rice**
- **Quick Cous Cous**
- **Golden Grits**
- **Fried Polenta**
- **Steel Cut Oats**
- **Outrageous Additions**
- **Tofu English Toast**
- **Pancakes with a Mix**
- **Orange Pecan Pancakes**
- **Fried Bread**
- **Scrambled Tofu**
- **Fried Mushrooms on Sourdough Bread**
- **Tangy Cabbage**
- **Maple Peanut Granola**

"'When you wake up in the morning, Pooh', said Piglet at last, 'what's the first thing you say to yourself?' 'What's for breakfast?' said Pooh. 'What do you say, Piglet?' 'I say, I wonder what's going to happen exciting today?' said Piglet. Pooh nodded thoughtfully. 'It's the same thing,' he said'."
A. Milne, **'The House at Pooh Corner'**

Symbols for making the best recipe choice
S = simple
A = adventurous
V = vegan
ST = Strengthening
R = Relaxing
C = cleansing
E = energizing

Hot Cereals

Here are four different hot cereals that are easy to prepare. I have added one more for the adventurous. The basic recipes are followed by a variety of suggestions to make your morning bowl outrageous. Each recipe gives enough for 2 mornings so you only need to re-heat on the second day.

Basic Oatmeal

S V R

Oatmeal is a great way to begin the day. Oats contain more protein, calcium and iron than other grains and also help to keep the heart strong.

Serves: 2 people

Cooking time: 10 minutes

Ingredients:

1 cup oat flakes
3 cups spring water
Pinch sea salt

Utensils:

Medium pot with lid

Preparation:

Place the water and salt in a pan.
Cover and bring to a boil on a medium flame.
Whisk in the oat flakes.
Cover with a lid and simmer on a low flame for about 10 minutes.
Stir from time to time to prevent sticking.
Extra water can be added for a creamier texture.
Remove from heat and serve.

Softly Rice

S V ST C

Softened rice is a great morning cereal because it is very easy to digest. It is also more relaxing than a drier grain. Umeboshi is an acquired taste because it is both salty and sour. Soft rice with umeboshi is a wonderful pick-me up for colds and digestive troubles or weakness and tiredness.

Serves: 2-3 people

Preparation and cooking time: 20 minutes

Ingredients:

1 cup cooked brown rice
2-4 cups spring water
1/2 umeboshi plum (optional)

Utensils:

Medium pot with lid

Preparation:

Place the cooked rice and 2 cups of water in a pan.
Cover with a lid and bring to a boil on a medium flame.
Turn the flame to low and simmer for about 10 minutes.
Stir occasionally to prevent sticking.
Add more water for a creamy texture.

Quick Cous Cous

S V R

Cous cous is a kind of pasta originating in North Africa. Rather than being in the form of noodles, couscous is rolled into tiny round granular shapes.

What is most appealing about cous cous, is its versatility. Once you have the basic recipe down, the things which couscous will do are limited only by your imagination. French couscous is very easy to prepare and can be added to boiling water and then removed from the heat. Whole wheat cous cous has to be cooked for 5 minutes. Both taste delicious.

Serves: 2 people

Preparation and cooking time: 5-7 minutes

Ingredients:
1/2 cup French or whole wheat couscous
1 cup spring water
Pinch sea salt

Utensils:
Small pan with lid

Preparation:
Place the water and salt in a pot. Bring to a boil on a medium flame. Add the cous cous.
Remove from heat and let sit for 5 minutes. If you are using the whole wheat variety, cook on a low flame for 5 minutes.
Fluff with chopsticks or a fork and serve

Golden Grits

S V R C

Cooked corn grits are also known as polenta. Corn grits are a light grain cereal. They have a cooling effect on the body and a mildly sweet flavor. I usually make enough corn grits for two days. The first day as a hot cereal and the leftovers are fried the following day.

Serves: 2-4 people

Preparation and cooking time: 15 minutes

Ingredients:
1 cup corn grits
4-5 cups spring water
Shiso powder for garnish

Utensils:
Medium pan with lid, skillet, whisk

Preparation:
Place the water in a pot and bring to a boil on a medium flame.
Whisk in the corn grits.
Simmer, covered with a lid, for about 15 minutes on a low flame.
Stir from time to time to prevent sticking.
Remove from heat.
Place half the corn grits into a rinsed dish. Leave to cool and firm. These will be used for the fried corn grits.
Serve the rest hot for breakfast garnished with shiso powder.

Fried Polenta

A V R E

This dish is made from the leftover Golden Grits. It makes for a great lunch or dinner grain especially when served with the baked beans.

Ingredients:
Pre-cooked firm corn grits.
2 tablespoons sesame oil
2 tablespoons corn flour
Shoyu
2 radishes finely grated

Utensils:
Skillet with a lid, metal spatula

Preparation:
Cut the corn grits into squares.
Roll in corn flour.
Warm a skillet on a high flame for a few seconds and add the oil.
When the oil is hot, add the corn grit squares.
Cover with a lid and fry for about 2 minutes on each side. Try not to poke at the grits because they will stick to the bottom of the pan.
Remove and serve hot with a little shoyu and grated radish

Oats have been known to develop an excellent sense of humor.

Steel Cut Oats

A ST V R

These oats are less refined than oatmeal and provide a steady, warming energy, which is great for vitality. Steel cut oats still have all the nutrients from the whole oat groats as they have simply been cut into small pieces. Steel cut oats are a rich source of soluble fiber, protein, and vitamins. This dish can be prepared the night before and then re-heated in the morning.

Serves: 2-4 people

Preparation and cooking time: 45 minutes

Ingredients:

1 cup steel cut oats
4 cups spring water
Pinch sea salt

Utensils:

Pressure cooker

Preparation:

The night before, place the oats, 3 cups water and salt in a pan.
Cover with a lid and bring to boil on a medium flame.
Reduce the flame to low and cook for about 15 minutes.
Turn off the flame and leave overnight.
In the morning, add 1 cup spring water, mix through and bring to a boil on a medium flame. Cook another 10 minutes and serve with any of the Outrageous Additions.

Outrageous Additions for Hot Cereals

Cinnamon Oatmeal
   Add 1/2 teaspoon cinnamon at the end of cooking and stir through.

Sweeteners
   Serve with a teaspoon of maple syrup or rice syrup.
   Strawberry jelly is delicious added to the oatmeal at the end of cooking.
   Maple sprinkles are a fun way to sweeten oatmeal.

Milk Alternatives
   Add 1/2 cup soy, rice or oat milk to the piping hot, cooked oatmeal. It will help to cool it down.

Nuts and Seeds
   Add 2 tablespoons roasted and chopped walnuts at the end of cooking.
   Sprinkle toasted and sliced almonds on top right before serving.
   Sprinkle toasted sunflower seeds over the oatmeal when serving.

Fresh Fruit
   Add 1/2 fresh apple diced.
   Add 1/2 cup chopped strawberries or raspberries and blueberries.
   Another option is to blend the fruit with a teaspoon of rice syrup.
   Add to the oatmeal after it is cooked

Dried Fruit
   Add 1/2 cup dried apricots and 1 teaspoon of rice syrup with the water and sea salt at the beginning of cooking. Bring to a boil and add the oatmeal. Cook as described in the basic recipe.
   Add 1/2 cup dried cranberries and 1 teaspoon maple syrup with the water and sea salt at the beginning of cooking. Bring to a boil and add the oatmeal. Cook as described in the basic recipe.
   Add 1/2 cup raisins to the water at the beginning of cooking. Bring to a boil and add the oatmeal. Cook as described in the basic recipe.
   If you prefer raisins uncooked, you can add them when you serve the oatmeal

Canned Sugar Free Peaches

Add a few slices of canned peaches at the beginning of cooking. Serve with Maple sprinkles.

For the Adventurous

Add an umeboshi plum at the beginning of cooking any of the cereals.

Add 1/4 cup finely sliced onion, 1/4 cup finely sliced cabbage and 1/2 cup finely grated carrot to the water at the beginning of cooking any of the cereals.

Add 1/2 cup of leftover beans and vegetables to the rice in the Softly Rice recipe. Add 1/2 teaspoon of diluted brown rice miso at the end of cooking. Cook for at least 3 minutes after adding the miso.

Tofu English Toast

A V R

It appears that a tavern owner in Albany, New York who was called Joseph French created the original French toast. So there is nothing 'je ne sai' pas about it. This is a vegan version using tofu and tastes fabulous too!

Serves: 2-4 people

Preparation and cooking time: 10 minutes

Ingredients:

4 slices sourdough bread
1/2 cake soft tofu
2 teaspoons mustard
1 tablespoon brown rice miso
1 tablespoon tahini
Pinch sea salt
1/2 cup spring water
2 tablespoons sesame oil

Utensils:

Heavy skillet, blender, dinner plate, metal spatula

Preparation:

Place the tofu, mustard, miso, tahini, salt and water in a blender.
Blend to a smooth paste.
Remove and place on a large plate.
Add the bread and let soak for about 2 minutes.
Turn the bread over and repeat soaking process.
Meanwhile heat the skillet on a high flame for a few seconds and add the oil.
When the oil is hot, reduce the flame to medium and add the bread.
Cover and fry for about 3 minutes.
Turn over and fry the other side for a further 3 minutes.
Remove from the skillet and serve.

Pancakes with a Mix

S V R

The only time I ever had pancakes as a child was once a year on Pancake Day or Shrove Tuesday. This is the Tuesday before Lent when all the rich leftover foods had to be used up. They were mixed together to form a pancake batter. The big thing is to toss the pancakes high in the air and catch them in the pan again. In France they have a Crepe Day on February 2 known as Chandeleur Day, which is the mid-point between the winter and spring solstice. Crepes were used because of their shape and color, which was likened to a candle. Mardi Gras celebrations also include a traditional dumpling in the form of a loose knot. So it seems that pancakes have a festive air to them and are fun for relaxing days and when a leisurely breakfast is called for.

Serves: 4 people

Preparation and cooking time: 15 minutes

Ingredients:
2 cups natural pancake mix such as Arrowhead Mills multi-grained waffle and pancake mix
2 cups sparkling water
1 tablespoon safflower oil
Safflower oil for frying
Maple syrup or rice syrup
Freshly sliced fruit such as strawberries or peaches
Roasted chopped walnuts
1/2 lemon

Utensils:
Large skillet, mixing bowl and whisk, metal spatula

Preparation:
Place the pancake mix, sparkling water and
1 tablespoon oil in a mixing bowl.

Whisk lightly to form a batter. Do not over-mix. You can even leave a dusting of flour un-mixed.

Let sit for 5 minutes.

Meanwhile, heat the skillet on a high flame for 10 seconds.

Add the oil and heat for another ten seconds.

Using a ladle, drop a small amount of the pancake mixture into the skillet to form small circles of batter. Add another pancake if you have space.

Turn the flame to medium.

Fry on a medium flame and wait until bubbles appear in the batter.

Turn the pancakes over and fry a further minute.

Remove and place on a serving platter.

Serve hot with maple or rice syrup and a squeeze of lemon. Garnish with fresh fruit and roasted chopped nuts.

Orange Pecan Pancakes

AVR

Serves: 2-4 people

Preparation and cooking time: 15 minutes

Ingredients:
1 1/2 cups whole wheat pastry flour
1/4 cup cornmeal (stone-ground, if possible)
1/4 oat flour
1 tablespoon baking powder
1 teaspoon sea salt
1 cup fresh orange juice
1 cup sparkling water
1 teaspoon finely-grated (organic) orange zest
1 tablespoon safflower oil
1/2 cup finely-chopped toasted pecans
Maple syrup or rice syrup

Utensils:
Large skillet, mixing bowl and whisk, metal spatula

Preparation:
Place the flour, cornmeal, oat flour, baking powder, and salt into a large bowl and whisk together well.

Add the orange juice, zest and water. Stir briefly, just to mix—lumps are okay. (This batter is a little runnier than ordinary pancake batter—the cornmeal really sucks up the liquid as it cooks.)

Let sit for 5 minutes.

Meanwhile, heat the skillet on a high flame for 10 seconds. You can add a few drops o f water and if they dance about and evaporate, the pan is ready. Add the oil and heat for another ten seconds.

Using a ladle, drop a small amount of the pancake mixture into the skillet to form small circles of batter. I like to make small pancakes, no larger than 4" across—vegan pancakes seem to cook better this way.

Add another pancake if you have space.

Turn the flame to medium.

Fry on a medium flame and wait until bubbles appear in the batter.

Turn the pancakes over and fry a further minute.

Don't overcook these—they should still be kind of puffy when they are ready. If you let them overcook, they'll go flat and won't be as light and cakey as they should be. Serve hot immediately with maple syrup and toasted pecans.

Fried Bread

S V ST E

Fried bread has been used throughout the world. In England we used to have it for breakfast with grilled tomatoes on top. In Poland they would rub slices of raw garlic over the bread after frying. Fried bread is very good for anyone who does physical work and is a rich snack for kids. It provides strong, active energy, which is good for any kind of sports and outdoor games.

Serves: 2-4 people

Preparation and cooking time: 10 minutes

Ingredients:
4 pieces whole-wheat sourdough bread
1 clove garlic cut in half
Safflower oil for frying

Utensils:
Pot for frying, plate covered with paper towels, mesh strainer

Preparation:
Cover the bottom of a pan with about 1/2 inch of oil. Heat on a low flame.
Cut the slices of bread in half.
When you are ready to fry, turn the flame to high.
Place a few slices in the hot oil and fry for about 1 minute on each side.
Remove with a mesh strainer and drain on paper towels.
Repeat with the rest of the bread.
If desired, rub a slice of garlic over the bread and serve.
Fried bread can be added to soup, or served with leftover beans and scrambled tofu. It tastes great by itself as a snack.

Scrambled Tofu

SVRE

A yummy way to serve tofu. Light yet rich and satisfying. A good source of vegetable quality protein. Great for breakfast, lunch or dinner.

Ingredients:

1 block firm tofu mashed
1 carrot rinsed and grated
1 celery stalk washed and minced
1 small onion diced
1/2 cup fresh/frozen peas
1/2-1 tablespoon umeboshi vinegar
1 teaspoon shoyu
1/4 teaspoon sea salt
1 tablespoon sesame oil

Utensils:

Skillet, wooden spoon

Preparation:

Heat a skillet on a medium flame.
Turn the flame to high. Add the onion and sauté for about 2 minutes.
Add the celery and sauté for about a minute.
Add the carrot and mix through the vegetables.
Add the peas and sea salt and continue to sauté for about a minute.
Add the tofu and mix through. Add the shoyu and umeboshi vinegar and continue to sauté for another 2 minutes.
Serve with hot brown rice and lightly blanched vegetables.
Scrambled tofu can also be served with steamed sourdough bread and tahini.

**"I went to a cafe that advertised breakfast anytime,
so I ordered French Toast during the Renaissance."
—Stephen Wright (American Actor and Writer, b.1955)**

Fried Mushrooms on Sourdough Bread

S V R

Serves: 1 or 2 people

Preparation and cooking time: 10 minutes

Ingredients:
1-2 slices whole wheat sourdough bread
2 cups button mushrooms finely sliced
2 tablespoons sesame oil
1 teaspoon shoyu
Few drops fresh grated ginger

Utensils:
Skillet

Preparation:
Warm the pan on a medium flame for about 10 seconds and add the oil
Add the bread and fry lightly for 1 minute on each side.
Remove and place on a serving plate.
Add the mushrooms and sauté for 2-3 minutes.
Season with shoyu and continue to sauté for a further minute. Add the fresh ginger juice and remove from the heat.
Serve on top of the bread.

Tangy Cabbage

S V R C E

Vegetables for breakfast may sound weird but they provide a bright and refreshing way to start the day. Lightly steamed vegetables are, uplifting and light on the digestion. You can steam lots of different vegetables like carrots, cabbage, broccoli, cauliflower, kale, Chinese cabbage, summer squash, winter squash, watercress or turnips. Double the recipe so you have enough for lunch.

Serves: 2-4 people

Preparation and cooking time: 7 minutes

Ingredients:
2 cups round cabbage finely sliced
2 tablespoons sauerkraut (optional)
1/2 cup spring water

Utensils:
Small pan with lid

Preparation:
Place the water and cabbage in a pan. Sprinkle the sauerkraut on top.
Cover with a lit and cook for 3-4 minutes on a high flame.
Remove from the pan and serve.
Other vegetables can be used instead of the cabbage.
Vegetables can be steamed together such as carrots, cabbage and sweet corn.
   If you are in a rush, cut the vegetables the night before and store them in the fridge.

Maple Peanut Granola

S V

Serves: 4 people

Preparation and cooking time: 35 minutes

Ingredients:

2 cups quick oats
2 tablespoons wheat germ, toasted
1/4 cup toasted sunflower seeds
1 cup toasted almonds, chopped
4 tablespoons sesame seeds
Pinch ground cinnamon (optional)
Pinch ground nutmeg (optional)
Pinch sea salt
3 tablespoons rice syrup
2 tablespoons maple syrup
1/4 cup peanut butter, organic, (no sugar added) creamy
1/4 cup raisins

Utensils:

Baking Sheet, bowl, storage container

Preparation:

Preheat oven to 400.

Place the dry ingredients and salt in a large mix and mix well.

Place the peanut butter, rice syrup and maple syrup in a pan. Heat on a medium flame. Stir until well blended.

Add the wet ingredients to the dry and mix together.

Place parchment paper on a baking sheet. Spread a thin layer of the granola mixture on the sheet. You might need two sheets.

Bake for 25 minutes or until golden. Stir the mixture half way through baking.

Remove from oven and cool on a large plate. Mix now and then while cooling. Add a small handful of raisins if desired.

Store in an airtight container.

Serve with rice, almond or oat milk.

Exercise

Cooking is the ultimate way to nourish the self. There is no getting around the fact that it does take time. Make a plan to block out a certain amount of time each day for cooking. Chose certain days when you have more time to make a larger meal. Instead of seeing it as a chore, look at cooking as a new hobby, a creative art, a form of meditation or a peaceful time to try new dishes, ingredients and flavors. The huge bonus is increased energy and the empowered sensation of taking responsibility for the self.

Between the Slices

There is something extremely gratifying about munching on a thick piece of bread with some delectable morsel on top. Bread has a long history and is probably the one food that is eaten by people of almost every race, culture, and religion. Wheat has been around since before recorded history when it was first chewed and then made into flattened bread.

In the past, a person's social station could be discovered by the color of bread they ate; the darker the bread, the lower the social station. Way back when, refined white flours were considered a delicacy because they were expensive to mill and more difficult to preserve. Today, we see the exact opposite of this trend with darker breads being more expensive and highly prized for their taste as well as their nutritional value.

The sandwich became popular in 18th century England where it was initially a food shared by men while gaming and drinking at night. It slowly became 'correct' in polite society as a late-night meal among the aristocracy. During 19th century England, the sandwich rapidly became popular with the rise of industrial society. It made for a fast, portable, and cheap meal that could be taken at almost any time of day.

Still considered the "staff of life", bread has been revered in religious ceremonies for centuries.

Early Egyptian writings urged mothers to send their children to school with plenty of bread and beer for their lunch.

Scandinavian traditions hold that if a boy and girl eat from the same loaf, they are bound to fall in love.

Menu:

- **Hummus Falafel in Pita**
- **Salad Sandwich**
- **Fish Fillet Panini**
- **Fish Stick Surprise**
- **Tempting Tempeh on a Roll**
- **Seitan Steak Sandwich**
- **Tofu Sandwich**
- **Tuna Spread**
- **Re-Fried Bean Burrito**
- **Veggie Burger**
- **Smokin' Salmon Sandwich**
- **Lemon Tahini Sauce**
- **Peanut Cilantro Sauce**

In the following recipes, feel free to substitute the suggested slices for your favorite breads, pita or wraps. If you have trouble with wheat, try spelt bread. This ancient grain is much easier to digest and can be enjoyed by those with wheat or gluten allergies.

The healthiest ways to serve bread are in soup or refreshed because the extra moisture aids digestion and assimilation. Sourdough bread is also more digestible than yeasted. The recipe for 'Refreshing bread' is in the Bare Necessities Section.

Hummus Falafel in Pita

S V R

The crunchy chickpea nuggets known as falafel can add an exotic flair and richness to your sandwiches. You can purchase them prepared at natural food stores.

Makes: 1 sandwich

Takes: 2 minutes

Ingredients:
Lightly refreshed whole-wheat pita bread
1-2 tablespoons tahini spread or hummus
4 falafel already prepared and steamed
Grated carrot
Minced watercress
Lettuce
Bean sprouts

Utensils:
Pan with lid, metal steamer

Preparation:
You can steam the pita bread and falafel in the same steamer.
Cut the pita in half and coat the inside of each half with hummus.
Add the falafel and salad ingredients.
Drizzle a little tahini spread on top and enjoy warm.

Salad Sandwich

S V R

This sandwich has lots of different options. I have listed some ideas for fillings below but use your creative juices to come up with some divine variations. You can change the bread for pita or tortillas, or make a wrap from a blanched collard leaf for an even healthier lunch.

Makes: 1 sandwich

Takes: 5 minutes to prepare

Ingredients:

2 slices steamed sourdough bread, pita or tortillas
Several leaves of various lettuces
Watercress
Grated carrot
Cucumber slices
Bean sprouts
Roasted red peppers
Peeled and sliced avocado
Grated granny smith apple
1-2 tablespoons peanut cilantro spread, tahini spread or hummus

Utensils:

Pan with lid, metal steamer

Preparation:

Steam the bread in the steamer for 3 minutes and remove.
Spread both slices of bread with your choice of spreads.
Pile a selection of various salad vegetables on top of one slice.
Top with another slice of bread.
Cut in half and enjoy.

**'Legend has it that whoever eats the
last piece of bread has to kiss the cook.'**

Fish Fillet Panini

S E

Makes: 2 Sandwiches

Preparation and cooking time: 20 minutes,
which includes 15 minutes for baking the fish fillet

Ingredients:

2 organic frozen crispy battered fish fillets
Thick slices of sourdough bread
Pinch sea salt
1 fresh tomato sliced
1/2 red onion finely sliced
1 tablespoon olive oil
Mustard
Tahini spread

Utensils:

Baking sheet

Preparation:

Pre-heat the oven at 400 degrees.

Place the fish fillets in the oven and bake for 15 minutes. In the meantime, mix the tomato and onion with a pinch of sea salt. Brush a little olive oil the bread. Place in the oven, oil side up for about 5 minutes.

Remove and spread the mustard and tahini spread on each slice of bread.

Place the tomatoes, onions, and fish fillet on top of one slice of bread. Repeat with the other slice of bread. Cut in half and enjoy as an open sandwich!

Fish Stick Surprise

A E

Makes: 2 sandwiches

Takes: 15 minutes

Ingredients:

4 organic Fish Sticks
1/2 onion, sliced
1/2 red pepper, sliced
1 tsp minced garlic
1 tablespoon olive oil
2 whole-wheat tortillas
Shredded lettuce
Salsa
Tahini sauce

Utensils:

Baking sheet, skillet

Preparation:

Pre-heat the oven to 400 degree.

Place the Fish Sticks in the oven and bake for 10 minutes. Place the tortillas in the oven for 3 minutes to warm through.

Meanwhile, heat the oil in a skillet and add the garlic, onions, and peppers. Sauté for about 2-3 minutes, and season with shoyu. Cook for another 2-3 minutes.

Place 2 Fish Sticks in middle of the tortilla, top with the vegetable mixture, shredded lettuce, and salsa. Drizzle a little tahini sauce over the top if desired

Tempting Tempeh on a Roll

AVE

Makes: 2 sandwiches

Takes: 15 minutes

Ingredients:

2 tablespoons shoyu
1 tablespoon brown rice vinegar
Few slices fresh ginger
1/2 package soy tempeh (4 ozs)
1 teaspoon mustard
2 tablespoons sesame oil
1 teaspoon nayonnaise (vegan mayonnaise)
2 sourdough rolls warmed in the oven or refreshed
Avocado, peeled and sliced
2 slices tomato
1-2 tablespoons sauerkraut

Preparation:

Place the tempeh, water, shoyu, vinegar, and ginger in a pan. Bring to a boil on a medium flame and simmer for 10 minutes. Remove the tempeh and spread one side with mustard.

Heat a skillet on a medium flame and add the sesame oil. Add the tempeh and cook about 3 minutes per side.

Remove from heat. Gently add 2 tablespoons of the tempeh cooking liquid to the skillet. Flip the tempeh once or twice until liquid is absorbed.

Slice the rolls in half. Spread the nayonnaise on both sides. Slice the tempeh into strips. Place the tempeh on one half roll and cover with sauerkraut, avocado, and tomato. Top with other half of the roll, gently press down and repeat with the other roll.

Seitan Steak Sandwich

S V S T

This sandwich was an inspiration from my great friend Helen Stevenson, who missed her steak sandwiches. She loves this vegetarian one even better!

Makes: 2 sandwiches

Takes: 15 minutes

Utensils: skillet, wooden spoon, tongs

Ingredients:

1 tablespoon sesame oil
1 medium yellow onion, thinly sliced
1/2 cup mushrooms finely sliced
1/2 cup seitan, thinly sliced
1 teaspoon shoyu
1 teaspoon balsamic vinegar
1 teaspoon rice syrup
1 tablespoon sauerkraut
Freshly ground black pepper (optional)
2 tablespoons shredded rice mock cheese (optional)
Lettuce
2 Whole-wheat rolls, sourdough rolls, pita, tortillas or 4 pieces of refreshed bread

Utensils:

Skillet, wooden spoon

Preparation:

Heat the oil over medium heat. Add the onion and mushrooms. Sauté for 3 minutes, or until soft.

Add the seitan and continue to sauté for 2 minutes. Stir in the shoyu, balsamic vinegar, and rice syrup. Add the pepper and sprinkle the shredded mock rice cheese over the top; if desired. Cover with a lid and let melt for a few minutes.

Spread each piece of bread with mustard and add a lettuce leaf. Place the seitan and sauerkraut on top. Place the other piece of bread on top and press gently. Repeat with the other sandwich. Serve immediately.

Tasty Tips

To preserve a wooden cutting board, rub with a thick slice of lemon. Add a tablespoon of olive oil, and wipe over the board with an unbleached paper towel.

Tofu Sandwich

S V R

Makes: 1 sandwich

Takes: 5 minutes

Ingredients:
2 slices refreshed sourdough bread
4 slices tofu
2 teaspoons mustard
2 teaspoons tahini
Few drops shoyu
Grated carrot

Utensils:
Pan with lid, stainless steel steamer

Preparation:
Refresh the bread in the steamer for about 2 minutes.
Place the tofu in the steamer and steam for about 3 minutes.
Remove and add a few drops of shoyu to each slice of tofu.
Spread each piece of bread with tahini, and mustard.
Add the tofu and carrot and enjoy as an open sandwich.

Tuna Spread

S ST E

This is a big favorite with my children and makes for a great lunch or picnic food.

Makes: Enough for 4

Takes: 5-10 minutes

Ingredients:

1 can tuna drained
1 small onion finely diced
1 celery stalk finely diced
1 tablespoon finely grated carrot
Juice of half a lemon
2 teaspoons olive oil
1 tablespoon tahini
1 teaspoon mustard
1-2 teaspoons shoyu
Pinch sea salt
Shredded lettuce for serving with the bread
4 slices steamed bread or 4 sourdough rolls

Utensils:

Suribachi, surikoji, small bowl

Preparation:

Place onions, onions, and carrot in a suribachi and mash well.
Add the tuna and blend together.
Add the remaining ingredients and mix well.
Serve on top of steamed bread with lettuce.
A quick version of tuna spread is to mix a can of tuna (drained) with 1-2 tablespoons nayonnaise (vegan mayonnaise), a tablespoon grated carrot, a little mustard, and a few drops of shoyu.

Re-Fried Bean Burrito

A V ST R

Serves: 4 people

Takes: 15 minutes

Ingredients:
1 can organic black (turtle) or pinto beans
2 tablespoons olive oil
2-3 stalks celery, chopped finely
1/2 onion, minced
1 teaspoon brown rice miso
1 carrot finely grated
1-2 cloves garlic minced
1 teaspoon sea salt
1/2 teaspoon chili powder
1/2 teaspoon thyme
1/2 teaspoon marjoram
1/2 teaspoon cayenne pepper
1 teaspoon balsamic vinegar
Freshly ground black pepper (optional)
1 scallion finely sliced
1 cup shredded lettuce
4 whole wheat tortillas warmed in the oven

Utensils:
Skillet

Preparation:
Heat a skillet and add the onion and garlic.
Sauté for 1-2 minutes and then add the celery and carrot.
Sauté for another minute.
Add the spices, beans, and water. Cook for about 5 minutes. Season with salt and miso and continue to cook for another few minutes.
Mash the beans and mix in the scallions, balsamic vinegar, and pepper if desired.

Place the beans in the middle of a tortilla and add the shredded lettuce. Drizzle a little lemon tahini sauce over the top and enjoy. Leftover rice can also be added. Shredded soy cheese or mock rice cheese can be sprinkled on top.

Veggie Burger

S V R

Makes: 1 roll

Takes: 8 minutes

Ingredients:

1 veggie burger
Few slices red onion
1 tablespoon grated carrot
Shredded lettuce
1 tablespoon Peanut Cilantro Sauce
1 whole-wheat roll
1 tablespoon sesame oil

Utensils:

Skillet, metal spatula

Preparation:

Warm the skillet and add the oil. Add the veggie burger and cover with a lid. Cook on a medium flame for about 3 minutes. Flip the burger and continue to cook for another 3 minutes.

Remove from heat.

Spread the peanut sauce on each side of a roll. Add the burger, onion and shredded lettuce and enjoy.

Smokin' Salmon Sandwich

S ST E

Serves: 2

Preparation and cooking time: 5 minutes

Ingredients:
1/2 packet smoked salmon
4 slices sourdough bread
1-2 teaspoons mustard
1/2 cup finely chopped watercress
1-2 tablespoons lemon tahini sauce
Capers (optional)

Preparation:
Spread the bread with mustard, and then the lemon tahini sauce.
Place slices of salmon on two pieces of bread.
Add the capers and watercress on top.
Sandwich with the remaining two slices of bread.
Cut into 4 squares and enjoy.

'Breaking bread is a universal sign of peace.'

Lemon Tahini Sauce

S V R

Tahini sauce is extremely simple and works well in sandwiches or as a salad dressing.

Makes: 1 cup

Preparation and cooking time: 5 minutes

Ingredients:
Juice from 2 lemons
1 clove garlic, minced (optional)
2/3 cup toasted tahini
1 teaspoon sea salt
1/2 cup spring water

Utensils:
Bowl, wooden spoon or suribachi and surikoji

Preparation:
Place tahini in a bowl. Add the garlic and salt, and mix well. Add the lemon juice, a little at a time, and blend well to create a smooth spread. If you want it a little thinner, add a small amount of water and continue blending.

Note:
A thicker spread is perfect for sandwiches, while a thinner spread can be drizzled over salad, vegetables, or served with falafel and used in pita, or wraps.

Peanut Cilantro Sauce

S V R

Makes: Enough for 4 slices of bread

Preparation and cooking time: 5 minutes

Ingredients:
3 tablespoons natural crunchy peanut butter
3 tablespoons fresh lemon juice
1 tablespoon fresh cilantro, minced
1 teaspoon shoyu

Utensils:
Suribachi and surikoji or small bowl and spoon.

Preparation:
Place the peanut butter in the suribachi or a small bowl.
Slowly add the lemon juice and mix well.
Add the shoyu and cilantro and mix through.

Exercise:
Try this great and delicious tasting sandwich. Spread 2 slices of refreshed sourdough bread with peanut butter, add a generous helping of sauerkraut and sandwich together. The combination is fantastic and nutritionally balanced because the sauerkraut compliments and aids in digesting the peanut butter and the bread. Better still, make it for a friend and don't tell them the ingredients. See what they think!

Soothing Soups

Treating a cold or fever with soup is an ancient and long-established practice. A bowl of soup, lovingly prepared, can make us feel soothed, nourished, and comforted. Soups are great for any season and are warming on a cold wintry day and cooling in the heat of summer.

Vegetable based soups have many health benefits. They are full of nutrients, low in calories, easy to digest, and gentle on the system. They help to calm our emotions and balance our energy. They are also easy to make.

Menu:

- **Luscious Lemon Broth**
- **Portuguese Potato Soup**
- **Lovely Lentil Soup**
- **Cool Lettuce and Pea Soup**
- **Minestrone Miso Soup**
- **English Onion Soup!**
- **Soothing Sweet Veggie Soup**
- **Fab Fish Soup**
- **Rice and Watercress Soup**
- **Vital Veggie Soup**

Luscious Lemon Broth

SVEC

A light, uplifting soup, which is a great for relieving stress and feeling relaxed. A simple detox for the liver too.

Serves: 4 people

Preparation and cooking time: 10 minutes

Ingredients:
1 cup Chinese cabbage rinsed and shredded
3 scallions rinsed and finely sliced
1 dried shiitake rinsed
Pinch sea salt
1/2 sheet nori toasted and cut into strips
1 inch strip kombu rinsed
2-3 tablespoons shoyu
1 tablespoon mirin
4 cups spring water
Lemon slices

Utensils:
Medium pan with lid

Preparation:
Place the water, kombu and shiitake in a pan. Bring to a boil on a medium flame. Remove the kombu and shiitake. Slice the shiitake mushroom and put it back in the soup. Add a pinch of sea salt.
Season with shoyu and mirin and add the Chinese cabbage, and scallions. Cook on a low flame for about 3 minutes.
Serve garnished with lemon slices and strips of toasted nori.

Portuguese Potato Soup

S V R

Soup is very popular in Portugal and they make wonderful variations with different vegetables and also fish.

This easy soup is a favorite with my kids and they often make it when they get home from school.

Makes: Enough for 4 people

Preparation and cooking time: 20 minutes

Ingredients:
4-6 potatoes peeled and diced
2 cups round cabbage finely sliced
2 carrots diced
1 tablespoon olive oil
4-6 cups water
Sea Salt
Black pepper
Parsley or cilantro for garnish

Utensils:
Medium pot with lid, potato masher

Preparation:
Place the potatoes in a pot and add the water. Bring to a boil on a medium flame.

Add a pinch of sea salt and simmer covered for about 10 minutes.

Add the carrots and continue to cook for another 10 minutes. Lightly mash the vegetables with a potato masher.

Add the cabbage and simmer another 5 minutes.

Season with sea salt and the olive oil.

Mix through and cook for 5 minutes.

Serve garnished with black pepper and a sprig of parsley or cilantro.

Tasty Tips

Thick and hearty soups are a meal in a bowl. Add a piece of fried sourdough bread at the bottom and enjoy with a side of freshly blanched vegetables for a superb lunch or an easy evening meal.

Lovely Lentil Soup

S V ST R

Serves: 4 people

Preparation and cooking time: 30 minutes

Ingredients:
1 cup red lentils
1/2 onion diced
1 carrot rinsed and diced
1 celery stalk rinsed and diced
1 cup sweet potato diced
4-6 cups spring water
1 tablespoon minced parsley
1 generous tablespoon brown rice miso diluted in a little water

Utensils: Medium pot with lid

Preparation:
Layer the onion, celery, sweet potato, carrot, and then the lentils in a pan and cover with a lid. Add enough water to cover the lentils.

Bring to a boil on a medium flame. Reduce the flame to low and simmer for about 20 minutes or until the lentils are soft. Make sure there is water always covering the lentils

Add the rest of the water. Return to a boil and add the miso. Reduce the flame to low and simmer for about 3 minutes.

Serve garnished with parsley.

"Soup for a healthy heart and soothed emotions"

Cool Lettuce and Pea Soup

S V R

This lovely light soup is refreshing yet substantial, and soothing; great in warm weather when a quick soup is desired.

Preparation and cooking time: 10 minutes

Ingredients:
1 packet fresh or frozen organic peas
1/2 head lettuce shredded
1 bunch scallions rinsed and cut into slices on an angle
1 tablespoon olive oil
Postage stamp size piece of kombu rinsed
1 clove garlic minced (optional)
Sea salt
Pepper (optional)
4-6 cups spring water
Mint for garnish

Preparation:
Heat the oil in a pan and add the scallions and garlic. Sauté for about 2 minutes and add the lettuce.

Continue to sauté for a further minute. Add the peas and enough water to cover the vegetables.

Add a pinch of sea salt. Bring to a boil and simmer on a low flame for about 5 minutes.

Remove from the flame. Spoon half the mixture into a blender.

Blend to a smooth puree.

Place the puree into a pan and repeat with the rest of the soup. Add more water if a thinner soup is desired. Heat on a low flame and season with salt and pepper

Continue cooking for a further minute on a low flame.

Serve garnished with mint.

**"An old-fashioned vegetable soup, without any enhancement,
is a more powerful anticarcinogen than any known medicine."
James Duke M.D.(U.S.D.A.)**

Minestrone Miso Soup

S V ST E

A hearty and nourishing soup that gives you warm, strengthening energy; great for lunch with some blanched vegetables or a salad.

Serves: 4-6 people

Preparation and cooking time: 15 minutes

Ingredients:
1/2 packet udon noodles
1 cup leek rinsed and sliced on an angle
1 cup cauliflower rinsed and cut into florets
1 cup hard winter squash diced in small pieces
1/2 cup cooked navy beans (canned or home cooked)
4-6 cups spring water
3 inch strip wakame
1 tablespoon brown rice miso
1 tablespoon white miso
2 tablespoons minced parsley

Utensils:
Medium Pan with lid, small bowl

Preparation:
Place the squash and water in a pan.
Bring to a boil on a medium flame.
Add the cauliflower and cook for about 5 minutes.
Add the leek and cook another 5 minutes.
Add the wakame. Break the noodles in half and add them to the soup along with the cooked beans.
Return the soup to a boil and add the miso diluted in a little water.
Cook on a low flame for about 3-5 minutes.
Serve garnished with parsley.

Tasty Tips

Look around and see if you can find some unusual bowls for serving your soups. Often thrift stores can supply some wonderful 'one off' bowls in different colors, with great rims, different shapes, clear glass or earthy and rustic. Start a collection and have your guests choose their favorite.

English Onion Soup!

AV ST R

This soup is rich and nourishing and helps you to feel relaxed and soothed whilst giving you inner strength and vitality.

Serves: 3-4 people

Preparation and cooking time: 35 minutes

Ingredients:
2 onions sliced into thin half moons
1 inch piece kombu rinsed
4-6 cups spring water
1 cup watercress rinsed and finely sliced
4-6 pieces mochi
1-2 slices of bread
1/2 teaspoon minced garlic (optional)
1 teaspoon sesame oil
Safflower oil for deep frying
2 tablespoons miso diluted in a little water

Utensils:
Medium pan, pot for deep frying

Preparation:
Place the sesame oil in a pan and add the onions.
Sauté for 2 minutes.

Add the kombu and cover with water and then add a lid. Bring to a boil on a medium flame.

Cover with a lid and cook for about 20 minutes.

Meanwhile heat the oil for deep frying the bread. (The full recipe for this is in the breakfast section).

Lightly fry the bread for about 1 minute. Remove and drain on paper towels. Rub each piece of bread with fresh garlic and cut into squares.

Add the miso to the soup. Add the mochi and cook on a low flame for about 3 minutes.

Add the watercress and serve garnished with fried croutons.

The soup can be placed in the oven at 400 degrees for about 5 minutes for a richer flavor.

Soothing Sweet Veggie Soup

S V R C

Pureed sweet vegetable soups are very relaxing and emotionally calming. They help to make you feel more satisfied and crave less sweets.

Serves: 4 people

Preparation and cooking time: 20 minutes

Utensils:

Medium pan with lid, blender

Ingredients:

1 onion diced
1 parsnip diced
3 carrots diced
4-6 cups spring water
2 teaspoons sea salt
1 teaspoon olive oil
(optional) Black pepper for garnish

Preparation:

Place the onion, parsnip and carrot in a pan and cover with water.
Cover with a lid and bring to a boil on a medium flame.
Simmer for about 15 minutes and add the salt.Simmer a further minute and remove from the heat.
Blend the vegetables in a blender.
Place the puree back in the pot and add the rest of the water.
Return to a boil on a medium flame and add the olive oil if desired.
Reduce the flame to low and add the parsley.
Serve garnished with black pepper.

*Other sweet vegetables can be used such as winter squash, round cabbage, or sweet potato.

Fab Fish Soup

A ST E

This soup is extremely strengthening and nourishing. When fish is cooked with vegetables it helps to create strong blood, and creates slow steady heat and energy in the body.

Serves: 4-6 people

Preparation and cooking time: 35 minutes

Ingredients:
1/2 pound white fish cut into chunks
1 large carrot washed and sliced on an angle
1 cup burdock washed and sliced on the angle
1 medium onion diced
1 bunch watercress washed and sliced
1 tablespoon sesame oil (optional)
1 heaping tablespoon barley miso diluted in a little soup stock
4-6 cups spring water
1-2 teaspoons fresh ginger juice
1-2 sheets toasted nori cut into strips
1 scallion washed and finely sliced for garnish

Utensils:
Medium pot with lid.

Preparation:
Heat the oil in a warm pan and add the onions.
Sauté on a high flame for 1-2 minutes and add the burdock.
Sauté for 1-2 minutes and repeat with the carrot.
Add enough water to cover the carrot and simmer for 10 minutes or until soft.
Add the sliced fish and simmer for
10-15 minutes or until the fish flakes easily.
Add the rest of the water and return to a boil on a medium flame.
Add the diluted miso, turn the flame to very low and add the watercress.
Cook for 3-5 minutes and serve garnished with ginger, toasted nori strips and scallions.

Miso

For century's miso has been made in Japan by craftsmen who transformed soybeans and grains into a rich, thick paste used for seasoning many dishes. Each miso has its own unique flavor, color and aroma depending on the region and people who prepare it.

Miso is now being made in America and there are different varieties such as white, brown rice, chickpea, and barley miso.

Miso literally means source of taste. It contains lactic acid bacteria and enzymes, which aid in digestion and food assimilation. It also contains a nutritional balance of vitamins, minerals, essential oils, and proteins.

Miso is a complete food and is very nourishing and revitalizing.

Miso is good for stamina, circulation, and digestion. It can help to strengthen the heart, blood, and immune system. Miso nourishes the skin and hair; so they glow with health. Miso can also relieve the effects of too much smoking, drinking, and environmental pollution.

Rice and Watercress Soup

S V ST R

When you use greens in soup, they add a light refreshing taste that makes the soup easier to digest and assimilate. Greens can be added right at the end of the soup preparation so they cook for just a few seconds. Try kale, collards, broccoli rabe, or Chinese cabbage. Leftover grains add substance to the soup and are comforting and relaxing.

Serves: 4 people

Preparation and cooking time: 10 minutes

Ingredients:

4-6 cups spring water
1 cup leftover rice
1 bunch watercress rinsed and finely sliced
1/2 leek finely sliced
1/2 cup dulse rinsed and finely sliced
1 cup fresh sweet corn removed from the cob
1 cup cauliflower cut into florets
1 tablespoon barley miso diluted in a little water
1 tablespoon sweet white miso diluted in a little water
2 tablespoons finely grated carrot

Utensils:

Medium pot with lid

Preparation:

Place the water and rice in a pot and cover with water. Bring to a boil on a medium flame. Add the cauliflower and simmer, covered for about 5 minutes.

Add the leek, simmer for 5 minutes and then add the corn. Add the rest of the water.

Simmer, covered with a lid, for 3 minutes and add the diluted miso.

Turn the flame to low, add the watercress and cook for about 3-5 minutes.

Serve garnished with finely grated carrot.

"Good soup is one of the prime ingredients of good living.
For soup can do more to lift the spirits and stimulate
the appetite than any other one dish."
—Louis P. De Gouy, The Soup Book (1949)

Vital Veggie Soup

S V R

Serves: 2

Preparation and cooking time: 15-20 minutes

Ingredients:

1 leek sliced
1/2 cup cabbage sliced
1 carrot slice on an angle
1/2 cup string beans cut in half
1/2 cup corn kernels
4-6 cups water
1-2 teaspoons olive oil
1 tablespoon cornmeal (corn flour)
1-2 teaspoons sea salt
Freshly ground black pepper
1 tablespoon fresh cilantro

Utensils:

Pot with lid, small bowl.

Preparation:

Place the kombu and about 3 cups of water in a pan.
Bring to a boil and remove the kombu.
Add the carrot, cabbage and leek.
Simmer, with a lid, for about 10 minutes. Season with salt.
Place the flour and oil in a small bowl and mix together.
Add the flour and oil combination to the soup and stir to blend.
Add the string beans and corn and simmer for 1-2 minutes.
Serve garnished with cilantro and black pepper.

Please note that any veggies can be used in this soup such as parsnips, turnips, onions, scallions, peas, kale, or cauliflower.

Exercise:

Use your creative flair and imagination to come up with your own soup. Dig around in your fridge and gather a selection of vegetables. Use oil and season with sea salt, shoyu or miso (not all in the same soup!). Add any leftover beans or grains. Use a little wakame and a dash of ginger. Write you recipe down and make notes about the outcome. Use any of the above recipes for inspiration and seasoning amounts.

Glorious Grains

Menu:

- **Shrimpy Rice**
- **Deep Fried Rice Balls**
- **Garlic Rice**
- **Nori Rolls**
- **Nori Rice Balls**
- **Millet Crush**
- **Asian Bulgur**
- **Broccoli-Barley Toss**
- **Cous Cous Pilaf**
- **Moorish Mochi**
- **Corn on the Cob with Umeboshi**

Whole grains are very different to refined grains. Whole grains are unprocessed which means they still contain their original constituents. Examples of whole grains are brown rice, whole oats, millet, barley, wheat, rye, or corn on the cob. Refined grains are those that have had the outer layers stripped and milled such as white rice, white bread, or pasta.

Whole grains are excellent for your health and contain numerous antioxidants as well as fiber, protein, and important vitamins and minerals. Whole grains are good for regulating body weight, strengthening the digestion, improving mental ability, and providing steady, enduring stamina. The energy of whole grains is both youthful and mature because each grain contains the seed, flower, and fruit in one. This means the complete growing cycle is present in each tiny grain. When we eat whole grains they help us to develop open, inquisitive, and flexible thinking.

Grains can be 40% of your diet. Check for other grain recipes in Bare Necessities, Brilliant Breakfasts and One Pot Cooking.

You can jazz up rice with toasted nuts and seeds, chopped parsley, mint, watercress or cilantro, or even make a zesty sauce to go over the top.

If you are in a rush use the pre-cooked brown rice that is sold in many natural food stores, and fry or steam it with vegetables to create a quick and tasty meal.

Shrimpy Rice

This is a wonderful way to use up leftover rice; rich, nourishing, and energizing. Please try to find organic shrimp so the harvesting is eco- and ocean-friendly. Vegans can use 1/2 block of firm, diced tofu instead. White fish is a great alternative to shrimp. Use 1/2 lb of your favorite white fish and cut it into small squares. Follow as directed in the recipe.

S ST E

Serves: 2-4 people

Preparation and cooking time: 10 minutes

Ingredients:

2 cups cooked brown rice
1/2 pound organic cooked shelled shrimp finely sliced
1 onion diced
1 cup broccoli rabe rinsed and shredded
Pinch sea salt
1-2 teaspoons shoyu
1 tablespoon sesame oil
4 cups spring water

Utensils:

Heavy pot with lid, steamer, pan

Preparation:

Place the rice in a metal steamer basket.
Place steamer in a pan with a 1/2 cup of water.
Cover and bring to a boil on a medium flame.
Simmer on a low flame for about 5 minutes.
Meanwhile heat a skillet and add the oil.
Sauté the onion for about 2 minutes.
Add the shrimp and sauté a further minute.
Add the broccoli rabe and sauté another minute.
Season with shoyu and cook another minute.
Remove from the heat.

Place a layer of rice in a serving bowl. Add a layer of the shrimp mixture. Repeat with another layer of rice and finish with a layer of the shrimp mixture.

Tasty Tips

Brown rice is a very versatile grain and can be used in many dishes. I like to make extra fresh rice and then use the leftovers to create new and satisfying dishes.

Deep Fried Rice Balls

A V ST E

These rice balls create high-energy and are good for intense physical activity, and playing sports. They can also help you to feel more out-going and positive.

Serves: 4 people

Preparation and cooking time: 10 minutes

Utensils:
Pot for deep-frying, small bowl

Note:
To test that the oil is hot enough, drop a small amount of rice into the pot. If it comes to the surface straight away the oil is ready. Try not to add too many balls at once because the oil will loose heat.

Ingredients:
2 cups leftover brown rice
Safflower for deep frying
1 tablespoon shoyu
2 tablespoons grated daikon
1 tablespoons mirin
1/2 spring water

Preparation:
Wet your hands and form a small amount of rice into balls, triangles or rolls. Make sure the rice is packed firmly.

Heat the oil in a heavy pot on a low flame until warm. Turn the flame to high when ready to deep fry.

When the oil is hot, deep-fry the balls until crisp and golden brown on both sides. This should take about three minutes.

Place the daikon, shoyu, mirin and water in a small bowl.

Serve as a dipping sauce for the rice balls.

Idea:

Other leftover grains such as millet can also be prepared and cooked as above.

Tasty Tips

If your garlic starts to sprout leaves don't throw it out. Plant the cloves in a small pot with soil. Place it on a window sill and watch the shoots grow. The tender young greens make a great garnish for soups, stews, or salads. Snip them and enjoy the faint garlicky flavor.

Garlic Rice

S V R ST

This is a traditional Portuguese dish that is very rich and satisfying and will have your guests wondering if you added butter.

Serves: 4-6 people

Preparation and cooking time: 1 hour

Utensils:

Heavy pot with lid

Ingredients:

2 cups long grain brown rice
3 cups spring water
3 cloves garlic sliced
1-2 tablespoons olive oil
1 teaspoon sea salt

Preparation:

Place the garlic and oil into a pan. Sauté on a high flame for about 1-2 minutes.

Reduce the flame and place the rice on top of the garlic. Add the water and salt.

Cover and bring to a boil on a medium flame. Simmer on a low flame for 50 minutes

Place the rice in a large wooden or ceramic bowl and gently separate the grains with the rice paddle.

Cover the rice with a sushi mat and serve.

"Rice is a beautiful food. It is beautiful when it grows, precision rows of sparkling green stalks shooting up to reach the hot summer sun. It is beautiful when harvested, autumn gold sheaves piled on diked, patchwork paddies. It is beautiful when, once threshed, it enters granary bins like a (flood) of tiny seed-pearls. It is beautiful when cooked by a practiced hand, pure white and sweetly fragrant."
—Shizuo Tsuji

Nori Rolls

A V R E

Nori Rolls are a traditional Japanese dish and make a lovely party snack. They are great for traveling, picnics or work.

Serves: 2 people

Preparation and cooking time: 5-10 minutes

Remember:
If you are making nori rolls in advance keep them rolled in the sushi mat to prevent them drying out. Cut right before serving.

Ingredients:
1-2 cups cooked brown rice
1 tablespoon brown rice vinegar**
1 teaspoon wasabi powder**
2 sheets toasted nori
1/2 Kirby cucumber, peeled, seeded, and cut into 1/16-inch matchsticks
1/2 carrot finely grated
1/2 firm-ripe small California avocado

Dipping Sauce:
1 teaspoon wasabi powder
1/4 cup spring water
1 tablespoon shoyu

Utensils:
Sushi mat, steamer, pan, bowls

Preparation:
Place 1/2 cup water in a pan and add the steaming basket. Place the cooked rice in the basket. Cover and steam for 5 minutes on a high flame. Remove the rice and place on a large plate. Sprinkle with brown rice vinegar and mix gently.

Place the wasabi and a teaspoon of water in a small bowl. Mix to form a stiff paste. Cover with a plate and let stand while making the sushi. (this allows the flavors to develop).

Place the sushi mat on a work surface with slats running crosswise. Place 1 sheet nori, shiny side down, on the mat, lining up the longer edge of the sheet with edge of mat nearest you. Using damp fingers, gently press about 3/4 cup of rice onto nori in 1 layer, leaving a small lip of nori nearest you and a 2-inch border on side farthest from you.

Arrange half of cucumber matchsticks in an even strip horizontally across rice, starting 1 inch from side nearest you. (You may need to cut pieces to fit from side to side.)

Peel the avocado and cut lengthwise into thin slices, then arrange half of the slices just above the cucumber..

Sprinkle half of the grated carrot across the cucumber and avocado.

Beginning with edge nearest you, lift mat up with your thumbs, holding filling in place with your fingers, and fold the thin strip of nori onto the rice to start the roll.

Roll the mat over filling so that upper and lower edges of the rice meet. Continue rolling and squeeze gently but firmly along length of the roll, tugging edge of the mat farthest from you to tighten. (Nori border will still be flat on the mat.) Open mat and roll log forward to seal with nori border. (Moisture from the rice will seal the roll.)

Transfer roll, seam side down, to a cutting board.

Repeat with the second roll.

Cut each roll into 6 pieces with a wet thin-bladed knife.

To make the dip, mix a little of the wasabi paste with the shoyu and water.

Dip the nori roll into the sauce and enjoy.

Other nori roll filling ideas:

Instead of above vegetables, spread 1 tablespoon of peanut butter followed by 2 tablespoons of sauerkraut across the pressed rice. Roll as above. Finely sliced dill pickles can be used instead of the sauerkraut.

Use 1 tablespoon of tahini and 1 teaspoon umeboshi paste instead of the avocado and roll as above. A strip of tofu can be added to this roll too.

Chopped shrimp mixed with a little nayonnaise (tofu mayonnaise) and finely sliced scallions makes a great filling.

"Nori Rolling"

Nori Rice Balls

S V ST C

Rice balls are like a small meal because they contain a whole grain, sea vegetable and a pickle. They help us to feel more grounded and balanced, and are very good for strengthening the mind, improving concentration, and increasing vitality. They are also a great way to use up leftover rice.

Rice balls are a great traveling, work, or picnic food because they are easy to transport and last for a few days without spoiling.

It you want to make them a little more exciting, try pan frying them after they are made.

Serves: 1

Preparation and cooking time: 5 minutes.

Ingredients:
Handful of cooked brown rice
1/2 sheet toasted nori
1/2 umeboshi plum
Water

Utensils:
Small bowl, plate

Preparation:
Tear the nori in half to make 2 squares. Place them on a dry plate.
Fill a small bowl with water. Wet your hands and take a handful of cooked brown rice.
Mold the rice into a flat wheel shape with your hands. Press evenly with both hands.
Press a hole in the center with your thumb.
Push the umeboshi into the center. Place a little rice over the umeboshi.
Continue molding the rice ball until the umeboshi is covered with rice.

Place the rice ball on one piece of nori.

Wash and dry hands. This step is important otherwise the nori with fall apart and stick to your hands and not the rice!

Fold up the sides of the nori so it sticks to the rice.

Place the other piece of nori to cover the rest of the rice ball.

Continue to mold the rice ball until the nori softens and sticks to the rice.

Place on a plate and serve.

For traveling, place in a brown paper bag.

Tasty Tips

Whole Grains are brown rice, millet, barley, sweet rice, rye, wheat berries, or oats, which:

- Give your brain and muscles energy, and strengthen digestion.
- Create, open flexible thinking.
- Are a good source of B-vitamins and iron.
- Help lose weight and maintain healthy weight levels.

Millet Crush

S V ST R

This dish is grounding and strengthening. The sweet vegetables help you to feel centered and in the moment. Makes for a lovely breakfast or lunch dish. Serve with a big bowl of blanched vegetables and stuffed cucumbers.

Serves: 2 people

Preparation and cooking time: 25 minutes

Ingredients:

1/2 cup millet rinsed
2 cups spring water
1 teaspoon sesame oil
1 cup cauliflower, florets)
1 cup winter squash or sweet potato cut into chunks
1/4 teaspoon sea salt
1-2 tablespoons sauerkraut

Utensils:

Heavy pan with lid

Preparation:

Heat a heavy pan over medium-high heat and add the oil. Sauté the cauliflower and the squash for 1-2 minutes.
Add the millet and cook (stirring frequently) for 2 minutes.
Add the water and sea salt. Cover with a lid and bring to a boil.
Cook for 20 minutes on a low flame.
Mix gently and serve garnished with sauerkraut.

Asian Bulgar

S V R

Serves: 3 people

Preparation and cooking time: 15 minutes

Ingredients:

1 cup bulgur
1/4 teaspoon sea salt
1 3/4 cups water
1 teaspoon minced ginger root
1 clove garlic finely sliced
Black pepper (optional)
2 scallions finely sliced
1/2 cup water chestnuts sliced
1 tablespoon shoyu
1 tablespoon sesame oil

Utensils:

Medium pan with lid, skillet

Preparation:

Place the water in a pan and bring to a boil.

Add the bulgur and salt and simmer covered for 10 minutes.

Meanwhile, heat a skillet on a medium flame and add the oil. Add the ginger, garlic, and scallions. Sauté for 1-2 minutes. Add the water chestnuts, cooked bulgur, and shoyu.

Cook for 3 minutes, gently turning with wooden spoon. Serve garnished with black pepper.

Broccoli-Barley Toss

AVE

Serves: 4

Preparation and cooking time: various

Ingredients:
1/2 cup hulled whole barley soaked in 1 1/2 cups water overnight
Pinch sea salt
1 cup broccoli cut into small florets
1 cup sweet corn
1 cup sliced mushrooms
1 scallion sliced
1/2 red bell pepper finely sliced
1/2 block tempeh
1 tablespoon mustard
1 inch strip kombu rinsed
2 tablespoons olive oil
2 tablespoons shoyu
1/4 cup water
1 teaspoon fresh grated ginger

Utensils:
Medium pan with lid, skillet

Preparation:
Place the barley, kombu and water in a pan. Cover and bring to a boil. Cook over a low flame for 1 hour.

Place the tempeh and kombu in a pan and cover with water. Add a tablespoon of shoyu, bring to a boil and simmer for 10 minutes.

Remove the tempeh and spread one side with mustard.

Heat the oil in a skillet and add the tempeh. Fry on each side for about 3 minutes.

Remove and cut into squares.

Place the skillet back on the heat and lightly sauté the mushrooms, pepper, broccoli, and corn. Season with the remaining tablespoon of shoyu and grated ginger.

Toss the tempeh and cooked barley with the vegetables and 1/2 cup water. Cover, and cook on a low flame for another 3 minutes. Mix and serve garnished with scallions.

Tasty Tips

Cracked grains are cous cous, bulgur and steel cut oats.

Cous Cous Pilaf

S V R

Serves: 4-6 people

Preparation and cooking time: 10-15 minutes

Ingredients:

1 cup whole wheat cous cous
1 1/2 cups spring water
Pinch sea salt
1 scallion finely sliced
1/4 cup fresh or frozen peas blanched
Few pieces roasted red pepper diced
1 cup cucumber washed and diced
1/2 cup diced firm tofu
1 tablespoon umeboshi vinegar
2 tablespoons parsley minced
Sprigs of mint for garnish

Dressing:

1 tablespoon olive oil
1 teaspoon sea salt
Pepper to taste
Juice of 1 lemon

Utensils:

Medium pot with lid, small pot for blanching vegetables, suribachi and surikoji

Preparation:

Place the tofu and umeboshi vinegar in a bowl and mix together.

Place the cooked peas, red pepper, cucumber, and parsley into a serving bowl and mix.

Place the spring water and sea salt in a medium pot and bring to a boil on a medium flame.

Add the couscous and cook covered over a low flame for 5 minutes.

Fluff the couscous with chopsticks and add to the vegetables.

Add the tofu and mix together.

Place the dressing ingredients in a bowl and whisk lightly with a fork.

Pour over the couscous and mix gently.

Serve garnished with mint.

Moorish Mochi

S V R ST

Mochi is sweet rice that is pounded to form a smooth, firm dough. Sweet rice is high in protein and vitamin B. Mochi can be purchased already prepared in a block and is very easy to prepare.

Moorish Mochi is wonderful for a quick and tasty breakfast or lunch.

Serves: 2

Preparation and cooking time: 10 minutes

Ingredients:
1/2 block mochi cut into 8 squares
1/2 sheet toasted nori cut into strips
2 tablespoons sesame oil
1 tablespoon sauerkraut
Few drops shoyu

Utensils:
Skillet with lid

Preparation:
Warm the skillet on a medium flame and add the oil.
When the oil is hot, add the mochi.
Cover and cook on a medium/low heat for 2-3 minutes.
Turn the mochi over and continue to cook for another 2-3 minutes.
If the mochi sticks to the pan, the heat might be too high or it is not ready yet.
Remove the mochi from the pan and sprinkle with shoyu.
Place a small amount of sauerkraut on the top of each.
Wrap a strip of nori around each square of mochi.
Serve hot.

Quick Meal in minutes
Moorish Mochi
Steamed winter squash
Stuffed cucumbers

Corn on the Cob with Umeboshi

S V C

The umeboshi adds a terrific, zesty flavor to the corn. A tasty combination of sweet, salty, and sour. Great for the digestion too.

Serves: 1

Preparation and cooking time: 5 minutes

Ingredients:
1 cob of corn with the leaves removed
1/2 cup water
Small amount of umeboshi paste or a plum

Utensils:
Pan with lid

Preparation:
Place the water and corn in a pan.
Cover and bring to a boil on a high flame.
Cook for about 4 minutes.
Remove and place on a plate.
Rub umeboshi over the corn and enjoy.

Exercise:

Have a sushi party

Cook up a pot of brown rice.

Have a number of sheets of toasted nori.

Cut up different vegetables like scallions, cucumbers, avocados, carrot, and watercress. Cooked fish, shrimp, slices of cooked tofu, or tempeh are great too.

Have nut butters, pickles, sauerkraut, and umeboshi paste on hand.

Make wasabi, and have shoyu ready.

Invite your friends and create new and wonderful fillings for your nori rolls.

Use Your Noodle

Pasta was first used as far back as the 1st century AD in Italy. This ancient food was not boiled like pasta but cooked in an oven instead. A very old Etrusco-Roman noodle was made from the same durum wheat as pasta today and called "lagane", which is the origin of what we call Lasagna. The Arab invasions during the 8th century also influenced the Italian cuisine. The dried noodle-like product they introduced to Sicily is thought to be the origin of dried pasta. The modern word "macaroni" comes from the Sicilian term for making dough forcefully; as early pasta making was often a very painstaking daylong process. By the 1300's dried pasta became very popular for its nutrition, and long shelf life; making it ideal for long ship voyages.

History claims that wheat noodles first found their way into Northern China in 100 AD and were imported from the Middle East. However, more recent discoveries have put the ancient wheat noodle as far back as 4000 years ago. We do know that noodle shops became the rage by the Sung dynasty. The Chinese rulers were the first to enjoy these delicious noodle dishes but they quickly became popular by other people due to the fact that noodles are nutritious, store well, are easy to prepare, and can be served hot or cold. This popularity has continued to grow. From China, noodles found their way into cuisines of most Asian countries: Taiwan, Vietnam, Japan, Cambodia, Laos, Malaysia, the Philippines, and Singapore.

Today most countries in the world enjoy pasta or noodle dishes cooked with many ingredients and sauces.

Menu:

- **Country Style Pasta**
- **Tofu Pasta Sauté**
- **Pasta with Tuna Sauce**
- **Walnut Pesto Pasta**
- **Mediterranean Noodle Salad**
- **Noodle Salad with Peanut Sauce**
- **Soba or Udon in Broth**
- **Pan Fried Noodles**
- **Cooling and Dipping Soba**
- **Udon with Sesame Sauce**
- **Luxurious Lasagna**

The directions for cooking great pasta and noodles are in the *Bare Necessities* chapter.

Country Style Pasta

Serves: 4-6 people

Preparation and cooking time: 15 minutes

Ingredients:
1 packet whole-grain pasta of choice
1-2 cloves garlic finely diced
1 onion diced
2 tomatoes diced
1 bunch basil rinsed and finely sliced
1 cup black olives cut in half
1-2 teaspoons sea salt
1-2 tablespoons olive oil
Fresh black pepper (optional)

Utensils:
Large pot with lid, serving bowl, skillet

Preparation:
Cook the spaghetti in a large pot of boiling, salted water for about 10 minutes.
Remove the spaghetti and strain.
Place the hot spaghetti in a large bowl.
Meanwhile, heat a pan and add the oil. Add the onion and garlic, and sauté for about 2 minutes.
Add the tomato and sea salt, and mix through.
Add the basil and gently mix. Remove from the heat.
Add the tomato mix and olives to the spaghetti.
Toss through and serve immediately.

Tofu Pasta Sauté

S V R

Serves: 2-3 people

Preparation and cooking time: 15 minutes

Ingredients:
1/2 packet whole wheat spaghetti
1 block firm tofu mashed
1 onion diced
1 clove garlic sliced
2 cups broccoli rabe
2 tablespoons olive oil
1 teaspoon sea salt
Fresh black pepper
1/2 cup water

Utensils:
Skillet with lid, wooden spoon

Preparation:
Cooked the pasta in a large pan of salted boiling water.
Place in a strainer.
Warm the skillet and add the onion and garlic. Sauté for 2-3 minutes.
Add the broccoli rabe and continue to sauté for another few minutes.
Add the tofu and mix through.
Add the water, spaghetti, and sea salt.
Cover with a lid and cook on a high flame for about 2 minutes or until the pasta is heated through.
Mix gently and serve garnished with black pepper.

Light Lunch:
Pasta with Tuna Sauce
Raw Salad with Tofu Dressing
Orange Mousse

Pasta with Tuna Sauce

S ST E

Serves 3-4 people

Preparation and cooking time: 15 minutes

Ingredients:

1 packet spaghetti
1 can 'dolphin safe' tuna
1 onion diced
Juice of a lemon
1 celery stalk diced
1 cup chopped parsley
1 teaspoon sea salt
1 cup spring water
1 tablespoon olive oil
1 cup green olives
Lemon slices for garnish

Utensils:

Skillet with lid, wooden spoon

Preparation:

Cook the spaghetti in a large pot of salted boiling water.
Place in a strainer.
Warm the skillet and add the oil.
Sauté the onion for a few minutes, and add the celery.
Mix through and add the tuna.
Sauté for another 1-2 minutes.
Add the water and bring to a boil.
Add the sea salt and lemon, and simmer for about 3 minutes.
Add the parsley and olives, and mix through the sauce.
Place the spaghetti in a large bowl and add the tuna sauce on top.
Serve garnished with lemon.

"Life is a combination of magic and pasta."
—Fellini

Walnut Pesto Pasta

SVR

Serves: 4 people

Preparation and cooking time: 15 minutes

Ingredients:

1 packet whole grain spaghetti cooked
1 tablespoon brown rice miso
1 cup walnuts
2 tablespoons tahini
1-2 tablespoons olive oil
Juice of 1 lemon
1 tablespoon brown rice vinegar
2 teaspoons sea salt
1 cup spring water
2 cups fresh basil or parsley

Utensils:

Blender, small pan, baking sheet

Preparation:

Pre-heat the oven at 300 degrees.
Place the walnuts on a baking tray and roast for 10 minutes
Place the walnuts and water in a blender, and blend to a smooth cream.
Add the miso, tahini, lemon juice, vinegar, oil, and salt.
Blend together to a smooth cream.
Add the basil or parsley, and continue blending. Add more water for a thinner sauce.
When the pesto is smooth, place it in a small pan. Warm on a medium flame to blend the flavors.
Serve over hot pasta.
Walnut pesto makes a great dressing for vegetables too.

Basil means 'royal' or 'kingly' in Greek and is considered a token of love in Italy.

Mediterranean Noodle Salad

S V R E

Serves: 4-6 people

Preparation and cooking time: 15 minutes

Ingredients:
1 packet spiral noodles cooked
1 onion diced
1 cup cucumber washed and finely diced
1/2 block firm tofu diced
1/2 cup minced basil or parsley
3 tablespoons umeboshi vinegar
1 cup black olives cut in half
1-2 tablespoons olive oil
1/2 teaspoon sea salt

Utensils:
Skillet, large serving bowl

Preparation:
Place the cucumber and tofu in a bowl, and add 1 tablespoon of umeboshi vinegar. Mix well and let marinate.

Place the onions, salt, and oil in a skillet.

Sauté on a high flame for 1-2 minutes and remove from the heat.

Re-rinse the noodles and place them in a serving bowl.

Add the tofu, cucumber, and onions, and mix together.

Add the rest of the umeboshi vinegar and mix through.

Let sit for about 5 minutes. Add more umeboshi vinegar if needed for a stronger taste.

Add the basil, toss through noodles, and serve.

Refreshing Supper:
Lettuce and Pea Soup
Mediterranean Noodle Salad
Hearty Steamed Vegetables
Blanched Broccoli with lemon squeezed over top
Appleberry Almond Sauce

Noodle Salad with Peanut Sauce

S V R

Serves: 4-6 people

Preparation and cooking time: 20 minutes

Ingredients:
1 packet spiral, wheel or penne pasta
1 carrot washed and diced
1 cup peas
2 scallions washed and cut into small rounds
2 cups broccoli washed and cut into bite size pieces
6 radishes washed and cut into quarters
2 natural dill pickles diced
1 cup mild black or green olives sliced
1 cup spring water
Spring water for boiling pasta

Dressing Ingredients:
1 tablespoon toasted tahini or sesame butter
2 tablespoons peanut butter
4 tablespoons umeboshi vinegar
1 teaspoon olive oil
Few drops shoyu
Spring water

Utensils:
Large pot for boiling pasta, small pot for vegetables, suribachi, surikoji

Preparation:
Bring a large pot of water to a boil on a medium flame. Add a little salt and a dash of olive oil.

Add the pasta. Cook for about 10 minutes, strain, and rinse well under cold water.

Place the pasta in a large bowl. Add the cucumber pickle and sliced scallions.

Place 2 cups of spring water in a small pan and bring to a boil on a medium flame. Blanch the carrot, peas, broccoli, and radishes separately in the boiling water; each one for about 30 seconds. Remove immediately and add to the noodles.

Place all the ingredients for the dressing in a suribachi. Mix well together. Add about 1/2 cup of water and mix to create a smooth dressing.

Toss through the noodles and serve.

Soba

Most soba noodles are made from buckwheat flour with unbleached white flour added. It is possible to get 100 percent buckwheat soba but these have a very strong flavor and tend to have a tough texture.

Soba noodles can be also be purchased with added ingredients such as green tea, jinenjo and mugwort, each one giving a unique variation to the flavor.

Soba or Udon in Broth

Soba in broth is extremely good for strength and vitality, and is helpful after a hard day at school, college or work when quick energy is desired.

S V ST E

Udon in broth helps you to feel relaxed and is a wonderful way to de-stress after a long day.

S V R E

The broth in this dish is saltier than a regular soup and is meant for flavoring the noodles. I don't recommend drinking all the broth, although a few sips are fine.

Serves: 2-3 rather hungry people

Preparation and cooking time: 15 minutes

Ingredients:
1 packet soba or udon noodles cooked for 7 minutes in boiling water and then rinsed in cold water
1 inch piece kombu wiped
1 shiitake mushrooms rinsed
1/2 teaspoon shoyu
1 tablespoon mirin
1 onion washed and finely sliced
1/4 block firm tofu diced
1 scallion finely sliced on an angle
1 sheet toasted nori cut into strips
3 tablespoons shoyu
4 cups spring water
Few drops hot sesame oil (optional)

Utensils:
Large pot for cooking noodles, medium pot

Preparation:

Place the kombu, shiitake, and spring water in a pot.

Bring to a boil on a medium flame.

Remove the kombu and shiitake. Slice the shiitake and put it back into the broth.

You can save the kombu and use it again in another dish.

Add the sea salt and onions and simmer for about 5 minutes. Add the tofu and bring the broth back to a boil.

Season with the shoyu, mirin, and hot sesame oil (if desired).

Turn the flame to low and heat gently for 2 minutes.

Place the noodles in individual bowls and pour the hot broth over the top.

Serve garnished with toasted nori strips and scallions.

Try mixing half soba and half udon for a great blend of flavors and energy.

Pan Fried Noodles

SVER

Serves: 2-4 people

Preparation and cooking time and cooking time: 20 minutes

Ingredients:
1 packet udon noodles cooked
4-6 cups spring water
1 carrot washed and cut into match sticks
2 cups Chinese cabbage washed and shredded
1 corn on the cob kernels removed
1 cup seitan finely sliced
1 scallions finely sliced on an angle
1 tablespoon sesame oil
1-2 tablespoons shoyu
1/2 cup spring water
1 teaspoon grated fresh ginger

Utensils:
Medium pot, skillet

Preparation:
Bring a pot of water to the boil. Break the noodles in half and add them to the water. Cook for 7 minutes. Strain and rinse under cold water.

Warm the skillet and add the oil.

When the oil is hot, add the carrots, and sauté on a high flame for about a minute.

Add the Chinese cabbage and continue to sauté for another minute.

Add the sweet corn and seitan, and mix through the vegetables.

Add 1/2 cup of spring water.

Place the cooked noodles on top of the vegetables and seitan, and season with shoyu.

Cover with a lid and simmer on a high flame for about 3 minutes.

Mix gently and serve garnished with chopped scallions and ginger

*You can use 2 cups leftover rice instead of the noodles

Bontio Flakes

Bonito flakes come from the bonito fish, which is a member of the mackerel family. These fish are known for their ability to preserve well.

The bonito are steamed, sun-dried, and wood smoked several times until they are completely dried. Then they are left to ferment for at least three months. The bonito fillets are shaved into flakes.

Bonito flakes are used to lightly flavor soups, noodle broth, and vegetable dishes.

Cooling and Dipping Soba

A E ST

This is a great dish for hot weather because it is very refreshing and at the same time gives you lots of energy. It is a good balance for raw fruit and salads.

Serves: 2-4 people

Preparation and cooking time: 20 minutes

Ingredients:
1 packet soba noodles cooked
3 cups spring water
1 inch strip kombu rinsed
1 shiitake rinsed
2 tablespoons bonito flakes (optional)
3 tablespoons shoyu
1 tablespoon mirin
1 sheet toasted nori cut into thin strips
1 scallion washed and finely sliced
2 teaspoons wasabi powder

Utensils:
Bowl for cooling broth, small bowl and plate for wasabi, skimmer

Preparation:
Place the shiitake, kombu, and water in a pan and bring to a boil on a medium flame.

Remove the shiitake and kombu. They can be saved for other dishes.

Put the bonito flakes in a small strainer or vegetable skimmer. Hold the strainer in the broth for about 2 minutes. Remember bonito are fish flakes and optional. Skip this step is you want a vegetarian broth.

Add the sea salt, shoyu, and mirin and simmer for about 2 minutes.

Remove the pan from the heat and place the broth in a bowl.

Leave to cool and then place the broth to chill in the freezer or fridge.

Place the wasabi in a small bowl. Mix the wasabi powder with a few drops of water to form a thick paste. Cover the bowl with a plate until ready to serve. This keeps the flavor of the wasabi.

Re-rinse the noodles and place on individual plates. Put the chilled broth in individual bowls and garnish with nori and scallions. Add the wasabi to taste.

Serve using the broth as a dipping sauce for the noodles.

You can use udon noodles for a lighter version.

Udon with Sesame Sauce

S V R

Serves: 4 people

Preparation and cooking time: 10 minutes

Ingredients:

1 packet udon noodles
Spring water
1 tablespoon shoyu
1 teaspoon mustard
2 tablespoons brown rice vinegar
1 teaspoon sesame oil or hot sesame oil
1 tablespoon mirin
1 cup spring water
1/2 teaspoon sea salt
2 tablespoons toasted sesame seeds
1 scallion rinsed and finely sliced

Utensils:

Blender, large pot

Preparation:

Fill a large pot with water and bring it to a boil on a medium flame.
Add the udon noodles and cook for about 7 minutes.
Drain the noodles and rinse well in cold water.
Meanwhile, place the shoyu, salt, mirin, vinegar, oil, mustard, and water in the blender. Blend well.
Pour the sauce over the noodles and serve garnished with toasted sesame seeds and scallions.
This dish is served cold.

Luxurious Lasagna

A R V

This is a great dish to take to a party or to enjoy with a group of friends. Substantial, divine, and satisfying. Wonderful for those new to vegan or macrobiotic cuisine. For a quick alternative, you can make this lasagna without the pesto sauce.

Serves: 6 really hungry people

Preparation and cooking time: 15 minutes prep and 45 minutes baking

Ingredients:
2 cups fresh mushrooms, sliced
1 teaspoon barley miso (diluted in a little water)
1 clove chopped garlic
1 tablespoons olive oil
1-2 26-oz jars of organic spaghetti sauce (or your favorite pasta sauce)
9 whole grain lasagna noodles
Soy Parmesan (optional)
Sliced black olives (optional)
2 tomatoes sliced

Tofu Sauce:
1 bunch watercress finely sliced
1 1/2 blocks extra firm tofu crumbled
1 generous tablespoon white miso
Few drops shoyu

Pesto Sauce:
2 1/2 cups basil, tightly packed
1/4 cup olive oil
1/2 cup macadamia or pine nuts (walnuts will also work)
3 tablespoons lemon juice
1-2 tablespoons shoyu or to taste
Salt and pepper to taste
Pinch cayenne pepper

Utensils:
Skillet, large pot, 9x12 inch dish or pan, blender

Preparation:
Bring a large pot to a boil and add the lasagna and a teaspoon of sea salt. Cook for about 5-7 minutes until they are al dente (not completely cooked). Drain and rinse quickly in cold water. Set aside

Heat the skillet and add the olive oil. Add the mushrooms and garlic, and sauté for about 2-3 minutes. Remove from heat and add miso and the spaghetti sauce.

Mix the tofu with the watercress, white miso and shoyu.

Preheat the oven to 375 degrees.

Place all the pesto ingredients in a blender and blend to a smooth creamy sauce.

Lightly oil the baking pan.

Spread half of the tomato sauce and mushrooms in the bottom of the pan. Place a layer of lasagna noodles over the sauce.

Spread half of the tofu mixture on the noodles.

Cover with half the pesto sauce.

Cover with another layer of noodles and then spread the remaining tofu mixture and pesto over them.

Top with a final layer of noodles, and pour the remaining tomato sauce and mushrooms over this.

Cover the dish tightly with foil, and bake for 30 minutes. Then, remove the foil and bake for another 10 minutes.

Remove from the oven and sprinkle with sliced tomatoes, soy Parmesan, and sliced black olives if you want.

Allow it to cool for 10-15 minutes before serving.

Exercise:
Buy a lovely recycled paper notebook. Start a menu diary to record your meals. Write down the menu before cooking. Look to see if you have a variety of vegetables, some oil, and protein. Maybe you need to add a dressing or have time to prepare a dessert. A menu book makes it easier to figure out what ingredients you need and which dishes to prepare first. It is also a great way to record what you are eating on a daily basis. Star some of your favorite meals or dishes to create on other occasions.

Perfect Protein

Menu:

- **Unchillin' Chili**
- **Bountiful Baked Beans**
- **Corn, Tofu, and Bean Salad**
- **Ginger Shoyu Tofu**
- **Sweet Miso Tofu**
- **Tofu and Veggie Stir Fry**
- **Batter Fried Tofu**
- **Sweet and Sour Seitan**
- **Mustard Tempeh with Olives**
- **Nutritious Natto**
- **Sweet and Sour Shrimp**
- **Marinated Fried Fish**
- **Citrus Fish**
- **Dijon-Dill Fish**
- **Tomato Basil Salmon**

Look for more protein recipes in the other chapters in the book.

You only need to have a small amount of protein on a daily basis, roughly 20% of you diet; this includes nuts and oil. Sources of vegetable protein are, any dried beans, edamame (young soybeans), tofu, tempeh, seitan, and natto. Fish is also an excellent source of protein and plays an important part in healthy eating. Fish contains plenty of amino acids, vitamins like D and A, various minerals, and essential fatty acids. Fish has an active and focused—but also calm—energy, and is very good for those who are on the go or play sports.

"Where's the Protein?"

Unchillin' Chili

S V R

Very relaxing and satisfying, Chili is easy to prepare and is lovely dish to share with family and friends on a brisk day in fall.

Serves: 4 people

Preparation and cooking time: 30 minutes

Ingredients:

1-2 tablespoons olive oil
1 onion diced
1 carrot washed and finely grated
2 cloves garlic, minced
1/2 red bell pepper diced
1 celery stalk diced
4 tomatoes diced
1 tablespoon tomato paste
1-2 teaspoons chili powder
1 (19 ounce) can organic kidney beans with liquid
2 potatoes peeled and cut into squares
1 teaspoon ground cumin
1 teaspoon cayenne pepper
1 teaspoon dried oregano
3 teaspoons sea salt
1 tablespoon balsamic vinegar
1 tablespoon fresh basil
1/2-1 cup water

Utensils:

Skillet with lid, wooden spoon

Preparation:

Heat the oil in a large saucepan over medium heat. Add the onions and garlic and sauté for 2-3 minutes.

Add the red pepper and celery, and sauté for another minute.

Add the tomatoes, potatoes, tomato paste, and carrot and mix through.

Add the kidney beans and enough water to half cover the ingredients.

Season with salt, chili pepper, cayenne, cumin, and oregano. Bring to a boil, and reduce heat to medium. Cover, and simmer for 15 minutes, stirring occasionally. Add the balsamic vinegar and basil and mix gently.

Serve with piping hot brown rice and lightly blanched garden peas and cauliflower.

Warming Winter Menu
Freshly cooked Brown Rice
Unchillin' Chilli
Blanched Cauliflower and Peas
Cool Cucumbers

Bountiful Baked Beans

S V R ST

Serves: 4 people

Preparation and cooking time: 1 hour 15 minutes

Ingredients:
1 can organic navy beans
1 carrot washed and cut into small chunks
1 stick celery washed and cut into 1/2 inch pieces
1 onion cut into large cubes
1 cup hard winter squash or sweet potato cut into cubes
Pinch sea salt
1 tablespoon shoyu
1 tablespoon umeboshi vinegar
1 tablespoon barley malt
Spring water

Utensils:
Pan, baking dish, wooden spoon

Preparation:
Preheat the oven at 450 degrees.

Layer the onions, celery, squash, carrot and beans in a pan. Make sure there is enough water to just cover the beans.

Cover and bring to a boil on a medium flame. Reduce the flame to low and cook for 15 minutes.

Add the salt, barley malt, shoyu and, umeboshi vinegar, and then stir through the beans.

Place the beans in a baking dish. Put in the oven and cook for 10 minutes
Remove and serve.

Louis Armstrong loved red beans and rice so much
he signed his personal letters thus:
"Red beans and ricely yours."

Corn, Tofu, and Bean Salad

SVRE

Serves: 4 people

Preparation and cooking time: 15 minutes

Ingredients:
2 cups cooked white beans strained
1 onion diced
1 cup sweet corn lightly blanched
1/2 block tofu diced
1 cup cucumber diced
2 tablespoons balsamic vinegar
1 tablespoon umeboshi vinegar
1-2 tablespoons olive oil
1/2 teaspoon sea salt
cilantro for garnish

Utensils:
Skillet, serving bowl

Preparation:
Mix the salt into the beans.
Mix the umeboshi with the tofu and let sit about 15 minutes.
Lightly sauté the onion in olive oil.
Place the beans, onions, cucumber, and sweet corn in a bowl.
Toss with balsamic vinegar and garnish with cilantro.

The flavor of fresh herbs comes to life if they are cooked quickly. Remember to add them at the end of cooking.

Ginger Shoyu Tofu

SVCRE

Serves: 4 people

Preparation and cooking time: 7 minutes

Ingredients:

1/2 block tofu cut into squares
2 cups spring water
1 small packet bonito flakes
2-4 teaspoons shoyu
1/2 sheet toasted nori cut into fine strips
1 scallion finely sliced
Grated ginger

Utensils:

Medium pan with lid

Preparation:

Place the water in a pan and bring to a boil on a medium flame.

Add the tofu and boil for about 2 minutes. The tofu will float when it is ready.

Remove the tofu and arrange on a serving dish.

Arrange a selection of garnishes on a plate; bonito flakes, grated ginger, scallion slices, nori strips, and shoyu.

Enjoy savoring the tofu with any, or all of the garnishes.

Sweet Miso Tofu

SVRE

Serves: 6 people

Preparation and cooking time: 10 minutes

Ingredients:
1 block tofu cut into rectangles
1-2 tablespoons tahini
1 tablespoon barley miso
1-2 tablespoons rice syrup
Finely cut scallions
1/2 cup spring water

Utensils:
Pan and steamer, small skillet

Preparation:
Place the tofu into a steamer.
Steam on a medium flame for about 5 minutes.
Remove and place on a plate.
Put the tahini and miso in a small skillet.
Heat on a medium flame and mix well.
Add the water slowly and continue stirring until it becomes smooth.
Add the rice syrup and mix through.
Pour the sauce over the tofu and serve garnished with scallions.

Tofu and Light Veggie Stir Fry

S V R E

This light and uplifting dish is perfect for a spring day or for helping you to feel positive and energized.

Serves: 2-4 people

Preparation and cooking time: 10 minutes

Ingredients:
1/4 cup snow peas rinsed and finely sliced on an angle
2 cups Chinese cabbage
1 cup bean sprouts
1/2 block firm tofu sliced into small squares
1 tablespoon sesame oil
Pinch sea salt
2 teaspoons shoyu

Utensils:
Skillet, wooden spoon

Preparation:
Sprinkle a teaspoon of shoyu over the tofu and mix gently.

Heat the skillet on a medium flame and add the sesame oil. Turn the flame to high and add the Chinese cabbage and a pinch of sea salt. Sauté on a high flame for about 2 minutes.

Add the snow peas and continue to sauté for another 2 minutes.

Add the bean sprouts and mix through.

Add the tofu, the remainder of the shoyu, and water. Cover and cook for 2 minutes. Remove lid and mix gently.

Serve hot.

Protein

Helps to build muscles, fight infection, heal wounds, and provides stamina and strength. Have some peanut butter, nuts, fish, tofu, or beans on a daily basis in your diet.

Batter Fried Tofu

A V R ST

This delicious way to serve tofu gives you a lovely sophisticated flavor. Deep fried tofu helps to relieve stress and gives you nourishing, deep and sustaining energy. A perfect dish for active kids too. Serve with hot, freshly made brown rice and lightly cooked vegetables for a simple yet satisfying meal.

Serves: 3-4 people

Preparation and cooking time: 35 minutes

Ingredients:
1 block firm tofu sliced into 1/4 inch thick squares
Safflower oil for deep frying

Batter Ingredients:
1 cup whole-wheat pastry flour
1/2 cup cornmeal
1 1/2 cups sparkling water
Pinch sea salt

Dipping Ingredients:
4 tablespoons shoyu
2 tablespoons mirin
1/2 cup spring water
1 scallion washed and finely sliced

Utensils:
Small but heavy pot for deep frying, serving dish, bowl for dip, bowl for batter

Preparation:
Place the tofu on paper towels to drain any excess moisture. Dredge each one with a little flour.

Place about 3 inches of safflower oil in a pot. Start on a low flame and turn it to high when you are ready to deep fry.

Place the flours and sea salt in a bowl. Add the sparkling water and mix gently. Do not over-mix. The marks of a good tempura batter are a powdery ring of flour around the sides of the bowl and a mixture marked with lumps of dry flour!

Place the tofu in the batter and coat well.

Place the tofu in the hot oil and deep fry until golden on all sides. This takes around 1-2 minutes.

Remove and place on clean paper towels.

Place the shoyu, mirin, water and scallions in a bowl. Place the tofu on a serving dish and dip in the sauce. Enjoy!

Tasty Tips

Remember that health is a direction, something that you move towards. The secret is to create a balance with everything you do: eating habits, exercise, work, play, relaxation, spirituality, and relationships.

Sweet and Sour Seitan

S V R ST

A rich nourishing dish that is perfect for cold weather. Seitan is made from wheat gluten and gives a steady, enduring energy.

Serves: 2-4 people

Preparation and cooking time: 10 minutes

Ingredients:
1 cup seitan finely sliced (you can buy this already prepared)
1 onion finely sliced
1 tablespoon sauerkraut
1 teaspoon mustard
1 tablespoon sesame oil
1 tablespoon mirin rice wine
1/2 cup spring water
1-2 teaspoons shoyu
1/2 cup fresh or frozen green peas
1/2 block mochi grated or cut into thin squares (optional)

Utensils:
Skillet, wooden spoon

Preparation:
Heat the skillet on a low flame.
Add the oil and then turn the flame to high.
Add the onions and sauté for about 1-2 minutes.
Add the seitan and sauté for another 2 minutes.
Add enough water to cover the bottom of the skillet.
Add the sauerkraut, mirin, peas, and mustard, and mix through.
Season with shoyu.
Place the mochi and top.
Cover and cook for about 3 minutes or until the mochi is melted.
Serve from the skillet with a side of freshly blanched broccoli.

Did you know that David Scott, the Athlete to win the Ironman Triathlon six times, was a vegetarian?

Tasty Tips

It is easier to change your diet if you have a partner in health. Find a friend who wants to eat well and enjoy the journey together.

Mustard Tempeh with Olives

AVR

Serves: 4 people

Preparation and cooking time: 15 minutes

Ingredients:
1 block tempeh
1 cup spring water
2 tablespoons shoyu
1 inch strip kombu rinsed
1 tablespoon mustard
2 teaspoons umeboshi vinegar
Safflower oil for deep-frying
Mild black olives
Radishes washed and sliced

Utensils:
Small pan with lid, pot for deep-frying, toothpicks

Preparation:
Place the tempeh, kombu, water, and shoyu in a pan.
Cover with a lid and bring to a boil on a medium flame.
Simmer for about 10 minutes.
Bring a small pot of water to a boil and add the umeboshi vinegar and water. Remove from the heat. Let the radishes sit in the vinegar for about 10-15 minutes.
Meanwhile heat the oil on a low flame. Turn the oil to high when ready to fry the tempeh.
Spread one side of the tempeh with mustard and cut into squares.
Deep-fry the tempeh for about 3 minutes or until crispy and golden-brown.
Remove from oil and drain on paper towels.
Serve the tempeh on small sticks with the olives and radishes.

Easy Evening Meal
Fried Polenta
Bountiful Baked Beans
Watercress Apple Rolls
Kool Kanten

Nutritious Natto

S V R E

Now this is a very weird food! However it is also a very powerful one. Natto is a fermented soybean product that contains living enzymes. Natto is wonderful for creating beautiful skin, improving digestion, and is know to relieve depression, strengthen the heart, and cleanse the arteries.

It is definitely an acquired taste but can quickly become a favorite. It is very easy to prepare and needs no cooking. The best way to start using natto is to add it to your miso soup or noodles in broth. A small teaspoon on freshly cooked rice a few times a week will quickly have you loving this stringy, strong tasting bean.

A normal portion is about 1 heaping tablespoon. Natto can be found in natural food stores and oriental supermarkets.

Serves: 1-2 adventurous people

Preparation and cooking time: 5 minutes

Ingredients:

1 container of natto (it usually comes frozen)
1 scallion finely sliced
1/2 teaspoon stone ground mustard
1 teaspoon shoyu
1/4 sheet toasted nori torn into small pieces

Utensils:

Small bowl

Preparation:

Remember to get the natto out of the freezer early enough for defrosting.
Place the ingredients in a bowl.
Whip together with a fork or chopsticks.
Serve over hot rice or with noodles in broth.

Tasty Tips

The shape of beans are similar to the kidneys and ears. Kidneys and ears have a special relationship and a similar shape. Beans are nourishing to both these organs, which govern vitality and balance.

Sweet and Sour Shrimp

A E

Serves: 4-6 people

Preparation and cooking time: 10 minutes

Ingredients:

1/2 pound organic cooked shrimp
2 tablespoons balsamic vinegar
2 tablespoons brown rice vinegar
2 tablespoons shoyu
1 tablespoon mirin sake or red wine
1 tablespoon rice syrup
1 tablespoon sesame oil
1 teaspoon minced fresh ginger
1 teaspoon minced fresh garlic
1 cup fresh or frozen organic peas
2 scallions rinsed and finely sliced
1 tablespoon kuzu diluted in a little cold water
1/2 cup spring water
4 cups cooked brown rice

Utensils:

Large skillet

Preparation:

Combine the shoyu, vinegar, rice syrup, mirin, and water in a bowl.
Warm a skillet on a medium flame and add the sesame oil.
Lightly sauté the ginger and garlic for about 30 seconds.
Add the shrimp, peas, and scallions, and sauté for about 1 minute or until heated through.
Add the shoyu mixture and the diluted kuzu and stir until the sauce thickens or for about 1-2 minutes.
Serve immediately on top of hot, freshly cooked brown rice.

Marinated Fried Fish

A ST E

Serves: 2 people

Preparation and cooking time: 15 minutes

Ingredients:
1 pound white fish such as fluke flounder
2 tablespoons shoyu
1 tablespoon mirin or sake
1 tablespoon brown rice vinegar or 1 teaspoon grated fresh ginger
1-2 tablespoons sesame oil
Small amount corn flour
Lemon

Utensils:
Large dish, skillet

Preparation:
Place the fish into a dish and cover with the shoyu, mirin, and vinegar.
Marinate for at least 10 minutes.
Remove the fish and cut it into three inch pieces.
Roll the fish pieces in a little corn flour.
Heat a skillet on a medium flame and add the oil.
When the oil, is hot add the fish and sauté for two to three minutes on each side or until the fish is tender and golden brown in color.
Remove and place on a serving dish.
Serve garnished with lemon.

Fabulous Fish Menu
Luscious Lemon Broth
Freshly Cooked Brown Rice
Marinated Fried Fish
Garden Salad with Tofu Dressing
Appleberry Almond Sauce

Tasty Tips

Make sure to buy fish that are sustainably harvested to protect the health of the ocean.

Mirin

Mirin is related to the rice wine, sake. Mirin is usually used for cooking while sake is usually served hot as an alcoholic beverage. The naturally brewed mirin gets its sweet flavor from sweet rice and koji. Mirin is an excellent addition to marinades, sauces, dips, fish dishes, soups, stews, and noodle dishes.

The mirin you buy in a natural food store is usually the better quality, naturally fermented product. Take care not to purchase those that are commercially brewed and seasoned with sugar.

Citrus Fish

S ST E R

Serves: 1-2

Preparation and cooking time: 15 minutes

Ingredients:
1 lb white fish such as flounder, tilapia, orange roughy, cod
1 tablespoon chopped cilantro
Freshly ground black pepper to taste

Marinade:
Juice from 1/2 orange
Juice from 1/2 lemon
1 tablespoon shoyu
1 tablespoon olive oil
1 clove garlic, finely chopped
Pinch sea salt

Utensils:
Shallow baking dish, small bowl

Preparation:
Preheat the broiler on high.

Place the marinade ingredients in a small bowl and whisk together.

Place the fish in a shallow baking dish. Rub a little salt over the fish.

Pour about half of the marinade over the fish. Keep the rest for later. Cover the fish with a sushi mat or clean dish towel and let sit for 10 minutes at room temperature.

Place the fish in the oven and broil, turning once with a spatula, until the fish is golden on the outside and flakes in large chunks when touched with a fork, about 4-6 minutes per side.

Remove from oven. Drizzle with the rest of the marinade, garnish with the chopped fresh cilantro, and serve immediately.

This basic recipe works well with any type of firm white fish. If your fish is thinner than 1-inch, reduce the cooking time slightly. If it is thicker, then increase the cooking time slightly.

Is it done yet?

To see if the fish is ready, gently poke it with a fork at its thickest point. Perfectly cooked fish is opaque and should be very moist. It should flake in large chunks. Fish that easily flakes and looks slightly dry is overcooked. Undercooked fish looks raw and translucent.

Dijon Dill Fish

SER

Serves: 2 people

Preparation and cooking time: 25 minutes (includes marinating time)

Ingredients:
1lb white fish such as sole, flounder, cod, orange roughy
Freshly ground black pepper to taste
Sprig of fresh dill

Marinade:
Juice from a lemon
1 tablespoon olive oil
1 tablespoon Dijon-style mustard
1 tablespoon chopped fresh dill or1 teaspoon dried dill
1 teaspoon brown rice miso
Pinch sea salt

Utensils:
Baking dish, small bowl

Preparation:
Preheat the oven to 450°F.

Place the marinade ingredients in a small bowl and mix gently with a spoon.

Place the fish in a shallow baking dish. Rub a little salt over the fish.

Pour about half of the marinade over the fish. Keep the rest for later. Cover the fish with a sushi mat or a clean dish towel and let sit for 10 minutes at room temperature.

Place the fish in the oven and bake for 6-8 minutes. Turn over and continue to bake for another 8 minutes or until golden on top and flakes in large chunks when prodded with a fork.

Remove from oven. Drizzle with the rest of the marinade, garnish with the chopped fresh parsley, and serve immediately.

This basic recipe works with any type of fish fillet. If your fillets are thinner than 3/4-inch, reduce the cooking time by a few minutes. If they are thicker, increase the cooking time by a few minutes.

"When you fish for love, bait with your heart, not your brain"
—Mark Twain

Tomato Basil Salmon

S ST E

Serves: 2

Preparation and cooking time: 20 minutes

Ingredients:

1 lb wild salmon
2 tablespoons olive oil
1 clove finely sliced garlic
2-3 tomatoes diced
1/2 onion sliced
1/2 cup green or black olives sliced (optional)
1 teaspoon dried oregano
1 teaspoon rice syrup
1/2 cup spring water
1/2 cup finely shredded fresh basil
1 teaspoon sea salt
Pepper to taste
Lemon slices for garnish

Utensils:

Baking dish, skillet

Preparation:

Pre-heat the oven to 450 degrees.

Place the salmon in a shallow baking dish. Rub a little salt and a tablespoon of olive over the salmon.

Bake in the oven for about 8 minutes.

Meanwhile, heat the skillet on a medium flame. Add a tablespoon of olive oil, and sauté the garlic and onions for about 30 seconds or until fragrant. Add the salt, tomatoes, oregano, water, and rice syrup, and cook for about 5 minutes or until bubbling. Remove tomato mixture from heat, mix in the basil, olives, and season with pepper. Place the tomato basil mixture on top of the salmon and bake a further 5 minutes or until the salmon flakes in large pieces when prodded with a fork. Serve immediately garnished with lemon slices.

Exercise:
Share a bowl of edamame (beans on branches) with friends. Buy a packet of frozen, organic edamame. They are young, green soybeans in a pod. Bring a pan of water to a boil. Add the edamame and boil for 2-3 minutes. Remove and toss with 1/2 teaspoon of sea salt. Serve in a big bowl. Use your teeth to pull the beans out of the pod. Discard the pod. Edamame are great for an appetizer or movie watching.

Vital Veggies

Menu:

- **Red Chili Squash**
- **Hearty Steamed Vegetables**
- **Minted Carrots and Peas**
- **Vegetable Medley**
- **Smashing Squash and Sweet Potato**
- **Sweet Daikon**
- **Saucy Cauliflower**
- **Sweet Arame**
- **Hiziki with Peanut Butter**
- **Cabbage and Sauerkraut Sauté**
- **Gingery Cabbage**
- **Garlic Broccoli**
- **Chinese Cabbage with Wakame**
- **Mixed Greens with Tangerine**
- **Watercress Apple Rolls**
- **Cool Cucumbers**
- **Stuffed Cucumbers**
- **Grape and Arugula Salad**
- **Garden Salad with Creamy Tofu Dressing**
- **Extra Dressing Ideas**

Check out how to blanch and steam vegetables in the *Bare Necessities* chapter

Eating vegetables on a daily basis has many health benefits. Vegetables are natural, living foods, and contain different vitamins, minerals, and thousands of other beneficial plant chemicals. Vegetables help us to feel refreshed, and positive, and provide lots of energy. They alkalize the blood, boost the immune system, add fiber, and reduce sodium intake. They are good for our skin, eyes, and hair, and are a great way to control weight.

Including vegetables into your diet is easy. Even if you are in a rush, it is easy to grab a bag of baby carrots, a salad mix, spread a little peanut butter in a celery stick or quickly steam some greens. In a pinch you can use a bag of pre-cut organic broccoli, and blanch it in minutes.

The following recipes are uncomplicated and contain a variety of round, root, and leafy vegetables, each one unique in energy, and effect on the body. The cooking styles are varied, and give you dishes that are strengthening, uplifting, energizing or soothing.

Remember that half of your daily food intake should consist of vegetables. Include some pickles during the week. Sauerkraut, dill pickles, and takuan (radish pickle) can be purchased in natural food stores. Only a small amount is necessary but they provide essential enzymes, which are important for digestion.

"Direction of growth"

Red Chili Squash

V S E

This is a fun and lively way to serve squash. Great with steaming hot rice and a bowl of lightly blanched greens.

Serves: 2 people

Preparation and cooking time: 20 minutes

Ingredients:
2 cups butternut or any hard winter squash cut into 1 inch pieces
1 medium onion diced
1 clove garlic chopped
1/2 teaspoon red chili powder
Pinch cumin
1 inch piece kombu rinsed
1 cup spring water
1 tablespoon chopped cilantro
1 tablespoon olive oil
pinch sea salt
1 teaspoon brown rice miso diluted in a little water

Preparation:
Place the squash and 1/2 cup spring water in a pan. Bring to boil on a high flame. Simmer on a low flame for about 10 minutes.

Meanwhile, warm the skillet, and add the oil.

Add the onion, sea salt, garlic, and spices, and sauté for 2-3 minutes.

Add the spring water and kombu. Cover, and bring to a boil. Simmer gently on a low flame.

Add the squash and miso to the sauce. Continue to cook together for another 3-4 minutes. Remove the kombu. Sprinkle with cilantro.

Hearty Steamed Vegetables

V R S ST C

This dish gives you strong, grounding energy; sweet and nourishing too. Perfect for cold weather.

Serves: 6 people

Preparation and cooking time: 25 minutes

Ingredients:

1 carrot rinsed and sliced
1/2 cup cabbage rinsed and sliced
1 cup winter squash sliced
Pinch sea salt
1/2 cup spring water
1 inch strip kombu

Utensils:

Heavy Pot with lid

Preparation:

Layer the kombu, then cabbage, squash, and carrot, in that order in a pot. Add a pinch of sea salt. Cover, and bring to a boil on a high flame.

Reduce the flame to low and cook for about 20 minutes or until the vegetables are soft. Mix gently and serve.

Minted Carrots and Peas

V S R E

This is a delightful, easy, and refreshing way to serve carrots. The pumpkin seeds add a wonderful texture, and extra nutrition, complementing the sweet taste of the carrots and peas.

Serves: 2 hungry people

Preparation and cooking time: 15 minutes

Ingredients:
3 carrots rinsed and cut in turned pieces
1 cup fresh or frozen peas
1/2 teaspoon fresh chopped parsley
1/2 teaspoon fresh chopped mint
1 tablespoon coarsely chopped toasted pumpkin seeds
1/2 teaspoon umeboshi vinegar
Few drops olive oil
1/4 teaspoon sea salt
Few drops shoyu
1/2 cup spring water

Utensils:
Pan with lid

Preparation:
Place the water, carrots, and sea salt in a pan.

Cover and bring to a boil on a high flame. Simmer on a low flame for about 10 minutes. Add the peas and a few drops of olive oil and shoyu. Continue to steam for another minute.

Remove and place the vegetables in a serving dish.

Add the mint, parsley, pumpkin seeds, and umeboshi vinegar. Mix gently and serve.

Vegetable Medley

V S R ST C

This dish is a treasure that is easy, delicate, and delicious, with the benefits of roots, round, and leafy vegetables in one. For a wonderful variation try steaming a piece of tofu on top of the vegetables to create a quick, clean, and healthy meal. Great with freshly, cooked brown rice.

Serves: 4 people

Preparation and cooking time: 15 minutes

Ingredients:
1 burdock root rinsed and finely sliced
1 carrot rinsed and finely sliced
1 cup collared greens finely sliced
1 medium onion sliced thick
1 cup cabbage finely sliced
1 teaspoon sesame oil
1/2 teaspoon umeboshi vinegar
Pinch sea salt
Few drops shoyu
1/2 cup water

Utensils:
Skillet with lid

Preparation:
Heat the skillet on a medium flame and add the oil. Add the onion and sauté for 2 minutes. Add the water and a pinch of sea salt.

Add the burdock, carrot, and cabbage and cover. Steam for 5 minutes on a medium flame.

Add the collard greens, and a few drops of shoyu. Steam for another 3 minutes.

Remove from the heat. and add the umeboshi vinegar. Toss gently and serve.

Smashing Squash and Sweet Potato

V S R C

If you are feeling stressed, this is the dish for you. Soothing, relaxing, and smooth. Make extra and turn the leftovers into a soup by adding water, a little wakame, and miso.

Serves: 4 people

Preparation and cooking time: 20 minutes

Ingredients:
1/2 winter squash peeled and cut in large pieces
1/2 sweet potato peeled and cut into large pieces
1 carrot rinsed and diced
1/2 granny smith apple peeled and grated (optional)
Pinch sea salt
1/2-1 cup water

Utensils:
Medium pan with lid, potato masher

Preparation:
Layer the sweet potato, squash, and then the carrot into a pan. Add enough water to cover the sweet potato.
Add a pinch of salt.
Cover, and bring to a boil on a medium flame.
Simmer on a low flame for about 20 minutes, or until the squash is soft.
Mix or mash with a potato masher until pureed.
Add the grated apple. and cook a further minute.
Mix gently and serve.

Tasty Tips

Examples of root vegetables are carrots, parsnips, burdock, and daikon.

Sweet Daikon

VSCR

Daikon is a great cleansing root vegetable. It is good for losing weight. Enjoy it with this rich and yummy sauce.

Serves: 6 people

Preparation and cooking time: 10 minutes

Ingredients:
6 pieces daikon rinsed and sliced thick on an angle
1 tablespoon tahini
1 teaspoon barley miso
1 tablespoon rice syrup
1 teaspoon finely cut parsley
1/2 cup spring water
1-2 tablespoons spring water.

Utensils:
Pan and steamer, small bowl

Preparation:
Place the daikon into a steamer.
Add the water and bring to a boil on a high flame.
Steam on a low flame for about 15 minutes.
Remove and place on a plate.
Meanwhile, put the tahini and miso into a small bowl.
Mix well and add the rice syrup. Continue to mix.
Add 1 tablespoon of water and continue to mix.
Add another tablespoon of water and mix to a smooth creamy sauce.
Pour the sauce over the daikon and serve garnished with parsley.

Saucy Cauliflower

VSR

A vegan version of cauliflower cheese. A great side dish for noodles in broth.

Serves: 4 people

Preparation and cooking time: 15 minutes

Ingredients:
1 small cauliflower washed
1/2 cup spring water
Pinch sea salt

Dressing:
1 tablespoon tahini
1 teaspoon mustard
1-2 teaspoons shoyu
1 tablespoon mirin
1-2 tablespoons spring water

Utensils:
Medium pan with lid, small bowl

Preparation:
Cut a cross in the stem of the cauliflower
Place the water, cauliflower, and salt in a pan. Cover with a lid and bring to a boil on a high flame.
Reduce the flame and cook for 10 minutes. Remove the cauliflower and place on a serving dish.
Place the dressing ingredients in a bowl. Blend to a smooth creamy texture.
Pour over the cauliflower and serve

Fats and Oils

Keep the hair and skin soft, give a feeling of fullness, and a nourishing, soothing energy.

Include some fat like sautéed vegetables, olive oil, nuts, or seeds at each meal.

Sweet Arame

V S R C

This is a soothing dish that helps you to feel grounded and secure. Arame is very good for cleansing the system, even of pesticides, or metal pollutants.

Serves: 4

Preparation and cooking time: 30 minutes

Ingredients:
1/2 cup dry arame rinsed and soaked in 1 cup water
1/2 onion sliced
1 carrot finely sliced in matchsticks
1/2 cup seitan finely sliced
1 tablespoon parsley finely sliced
1-2 teaspoons shoyu
1-2 teaspoons sesame oil

Utensils:
Small skillet with lid

Preparation:
Warm the skillet and add the oil.
Add the onion and sauté for 2 minutes.
Drain the arame. You can save the soaking water to use in the dish or for watering plants.
Layer the arame, carrots and then the seitan on top of the onions.
Add enough water to cover the arame.
Cover with a lid and bring to a boil.
Reduce the flame to medium and simmer for 15 minutes.
Season with shoyu and simmer another 5 minutes. If there is still a lot of liquid, remove the lid and cook on a high flame for 5 minutes longer.
Mix gently and sprinkle with chopped parsley.

Tasty Tips

Examples of round vegetables are squash, turnips, cabbage, rutabaga, cauliflower, radishes, and onions

Hiziki with Peanut Butter

V S ST C

This is a big favorite in my family. Easy to prepare, packed with minerals, and a fab blend of flavors.

Serves: 4-6 people

Preparation and cooking time: 40 minutes/10 min. soaking

Ingredients:
1/2 packet hiziki rinsed and soaked for10 minutes
1-2 tablespoons peanut butter
2 tablespoons sauerkraut
Spring water
1 teaspoon shoyu

Utensils:
Medium pan with lid

Preparation:
Place the hijiki in a pan. Discard the soaking water because it is too strong tasting. (You can use it for watering plants.)

Add enough water to just cover the hiziki. Cover, and bring to a boil on a medium flame.

Reduce the flame to medium low flame and simmer for 20 minutes.

Season with shoyu.

Add the peanut butter in small pieces.

Simmer for 10 minutes and mix gently.

If there is an excess of water, remove lid and simmer on a medium high flame for 5 minutes.

Add the sauerkraut, mix gently and serve

Light Soothing Supper
Udon in Broth
Sweet Miso Tofu
Cabbage and Sauerkraut Sauté

Cabbage and Sauerkraut Sauté

V S C E

Sauerkraut has incredible properties. Great for the digestion, weight loss, and cleansing the system. This sweet and sour dish makes you feel uplifted yet centered at the same time.

Serves: 2 people

Preparation and cooking time: 7 minutes

Ingredients:
2 cups white cabbage rinsed and shredded
3 tablespoons sauerkraut
1 teaspoon sesame oil
1/2 cup spring water
Pinch sea salt

Utensils:

Skillet with lid

Preparation:
Warm the skillet and add the oil.
Sauté the cabbage on a high flame for 2 minutes.
Add the water and cover. Simmer for 3-4 minutes.
Add the sauerkraut. Mix gently and serve.

Takuan is a pickle that can be purchased in natural food stores. Takuan pickles date back to the Japanese feudal period where they were made by vegetarian monks. They are made from whole daikon that is pickled in a rice bran mix for at least 3 months. These pickles are very strengthening and warming. They provide essential enzymes, and are great for digestion. Once opened, store the pickle in a glass jar in the fridge. Serve a few very finely sliced pieces at the end of your meal. Takuan is also delicious when sautéed with vegetables or added to cooked greens.

Gingery Cabbage

S V E

This quick and easy recipe is a great way to enjoy cabbage in just a few minutes.

Serves: 2 hungry people

Preparation and cooking time: 15 minutes

Ingredients:
2 cups white cabbage shredded
1 scallion finely sliced
1 teaspoon minced fresh ginger
1 teaspoon sesame oil
1 teaspoon shoyu
1 tablespoon brown rice vinegar
Pinch sea salt

Utensils:

Skillet

Preparation:
Warm the skillet and add the oil.

Sauté the cabbage, scallion, sea salt, and ginger over a medium heat for 3-4 minutes, stirring frequently.

Add the shoyu and brown rice vinegar. Continue to sauté for another 2 minutes.

Serve from the skillet.

Garlic Broccoli

SVER

A light, uplifting and refreshing way to serve broccoli or other greens, perfect for feeling positive, and refreshed.

Serves: 2 hungry people

Preparation and cooking time: 10 minutes

Ingredients:
2 cups broccoli washed and cut into small florets (dice the stems)*
1 tablespoon olive oil
1/2 teaspoon sea salt
1 clove garlic sliced
1/2 cup water

*Other green such as watercress, kale, collards, or broccoli rabe can be used instead of broccoli

Utensils:
Skillet with lid

Preparation:
Warm a skillet on a medium flame.
Add the olive oil and turn the flame to high.
Add the broccoli, garlic, and sea salt.
Sauté the broccoli until coated in oil; about 1-2 minutes.
Add the water and cover with a lid. Steam for another 2 minutes.
Remove the lid, mix gently and serve.

Tasty Tips

Examples of upward leafy vegetables are; Chinese cabbage, collards, watercress, leeks, chives, scallions, kale, mustard greens, broccoli, broccoli rabe, lettuce, arugula

Chinese Cabbage with Wakame

VSEC

A light and refreshing dish; wakame adds minerals, and is good for weight loss, and improves thinking and memory.

Serves: 2 people

Preparation and cooking time: 10 minutes

Ingredients:
3 cups Chinese cabbage rinsed and finely sliced
1 tablespoon wakame flakes rinsed
1 teaspoon shoyu
Pinch sea salt
1 tablespoon sesame oil

Preparation:
Warm the skillet and add the oil. Turn the flame to high and add the Chinese cabbage, and sea salt; sauté for 3 minutes.

Add the wakame and sauté for 2 minutes. Season with shoyu and continue cook for another minute.

Mixed Greens with Tangerine Dressing

VSEC

The combination of greens, and dulse packs a punch on the iron front. Full of nutrients with an added twist of tangerine. Great served with a bowl of hot noodles in broth.

Serves: 4 people

Preparation and cooking time: 10 minutes

Ingredients:
1 bunch watercress washed and sliced
1 cup kale rinsed and finely sliced
1 cup collards rinsed and finely sliced
1 tablespoon dried dulse rinsed and sliced
Juice from 2 tangerines or 1 orange
Few drops olive oil
1 teaspoon shoyu
1 tablespoon roasted and chopped almonds

Utensils:
Medium pan with lid

Preparation:
Bring a pot of water to a boil on a medium flame. Turn the flame to high. Blanch the kale and collards for about 1-2 minutes. Remove and place in a serving bowl. Bring the water back to a boil. Add the watercress and blanch for about 10 seconds.

Remove and add to the other greens.

Add the dulse and mix through the vegetables. Mix the shoyu, olive oil and tangerine juice together and pour over the greens. Sprinkle with toasted almonds and serve.

Tasty Tips

The tops from root vegetables such as carrots, turnips, or daikon are a wonderful source of nutrients. Try steaming them together with their roots. The combination of the whole vegetable gives you a wonderful feeling of completeness, and is excellent for both the lower body and digestion, and the upper body and lungs.

Watercress Apple Rolls

VSEC

This is a simple way to prepare greens that gives a light, elegant appearance. Green rolls are also a great way to take vegetables when traveling because they are easy to pack and eat with fingers. Flying can be a dehydrating experience. A small container of green rolls can help you to feel refreshed during your flight.

Serves: 2 people

Preparation and cooking time: 10 minutes

Ingredients:
I bunch watercress
1/4 granny smith apple finely sliced
Grated carrot for garnish
2 cups water

Utensils:
Pot for blanching, sushi mat

Preparation:
Bring the water to a boil. Add the watercress and blanch for 10 seconds. Remove and place on a plate.
Place the watercress across the sushi mat.
Place a line of apples along the greens.
Roll up the greens in the sushi mat. Gently squeeze out the excess water.
Unroll the sushi mat and cut the watercress into small rounds.
Stand the rolls up so the apples show and garnish the tops with grated carrot.

Cool Cucumbers

V S E

Cucumbers help to cool the body and eliminate excess salt.

Serves: 2 very hungry people

Preparation and cooking time: 5 minutes with 10 minutes marinating

Ingredients:
1 English seedless cucumber peeled and cut on an angle
1/2 teaspoon sea salt
1 tablespoon brown rice vinegar

Utensils:
Small serving bowl

Preparation:
Place the cucumbers and sea salt in a bowl. Mix gently.
Let sit for at least 10 minutes.
Add the brown rice vinegar, mix gently and serve.

Tasty Tips

Watercress is a fast growing plant that thrives in water. It contains high levels of iron, calcium, and folic acid; as well as vitamins A and C. It is thought to be one of the oldest known leaf vegetables to be eaten by humans.

Stuffed Cucumbers

V S E

This is so easy yet looks fabulous and makes for a great appetizer, snack or side dish in a meal.

Serves: 4 people

Preparation and cooking time: 5 minutes with 15 minutes to marinate

Ingredients:
1 English seedless cucumber peeled
1/4 block firm tofu mashed
1 tablespoon umeboshi vinegar
Few drops shoyu

Preparation:
Mix the tofu, umeboshi vinegar, and shoyu together.
Cut the cucumber in half lengthwise.
Scoop out the middle of the cucumber with a teaspoon.
Stuff the center of the cucumber with the tofu mixture.
Leave to sit for at least 15 minutes.
Slice into bite size pieces and enjoy.

Tasty Tips

Vining plants include; cucumbers, string beans, peas, summer squash, zucchini

Grape and Arugula Salad

V S R

Serves: about 3 people

Preparation and cooking time: 10 minutes

Ingredients:
1/2 cup seedless green grapes rinsed and sliced in half
1/2 bag arugula rinsed (2 cups)
1 cup cucumber peeled and finely sliced
1 teaspoon extra virgin olive oil
1 tablespoon fresh lemon juice
1/4 teaspoon sea salt
Cracked black pepper to taste
1/4 block of firm tofu diced
1 teaspoon umeboshi vinegar

Utensils:
Small bowls, serving dish

Preparation:
Place the rinsed arugula on paper towels to dry.
Mix the tofu with the umeboshi vinegar and marinate for 10 minutes.
Place the arugula, cucumbers, and grapes into a bowl.
Mix the lemon, sea salt, and olive oil in a bowl.
Add the tofu to the salad and mix gently.
Just before serving drizzle the salad with the dressing and a little black pepper (optional).

Garden Salad with Creamy Tofu Dressing

V S R

Tofu dressing is easy to make and can be used as a sauce for noodles, or a dip for blanched or steamed vegetables.

Serves: 4 people

Preparation and cooking time: 15 minutes

Ingredients:
1/2 head iceberg lettuce washed and torn into pieces
1 carrot washed and grated
1 cucumber washed and finely sliced
1 cup fresh corn kernels
1 cup fresh peas
5 kale leaves washed and finely sliced
1 cup chickpeas
1/2 teaspoon sea salt

Tofu Dressing Ingredients:
1/2 block tofu
1 heaping teaspoon umeboshi paste
2 teaspoons brown rice vinegar
1 teaspoon mirin
1 teaspoon shoyu
1/2-1 cup water

Utensils:
Serving bowl with plate and weight, blender

Preparation:
Place the lettuce, carrot, and cucumber in a bowl, and lightly toss the salt through the vegetables.
Lightly blanch the corn, peas, and then kale. Allow to cool.
Add the vegetables and chickpeas to the salad ingredients and mix gently.

Meanwhile, place the dressing ingredients in blender, and blend to a smooth cream.

Add more water for a thinner consistency.

Place in a jug and serve with the salad.

Tasty Tips

Suribachi - This is a great tool for the kitchen. It is a deep bowl with ridged sides, which makes it easy to grind seeds, and make dressings in small quantities.

Surikoji is the wooden pestle that is used with a suribachi.

Extra Dressing Ideas

An easy way to mix a dressing is to put it in a jar with a lid. Make sure the lid is on tightly and shake vigorously for a minute. Pour into a small bowl and serve. By the way, this only works with liquid ingredients.

Squeeze lemon or brown rice vinegar over blanched, steamed, or raw vegetables. Lemon squeezed over cooked greens is very helpful for cleansing the liver.

Mix 1 tablespoon umeboshi vinegar with a few drops of olive oil, and a tablespoon of water.

Mix 1 tablespoon umeboshi vinegar with a few drops of olive oil, 1 teaspoon mustard, and a tablespoon water.

Mix 1 tablespoon each of brown rice vinegar and spring water, 1 teaspoon of shoyu, 1 teaspoon mirin, and a teaspoon sesame oil. Great over noodles or fish.

Mix 2 tablespoons balsamic vinegar, 1 teaspoon chopped parsley, 1 tablespoon water, 1 teaspoon olive oil, 1/2 teaspoon sea salt.

Mix 1 tablespoon peanut butter, 1 teaspoon umeboshi vinegar, few drops shoyu, 2 tablespoons water.

Mix 1 tablespoon tahini, 1 tablespoon brown rice vinegar, 1 teaspoon shoyu, 2 tablespoons spring water.

Mix 1 tablespoon tahini, 1 tablespoon brown rice vinegar, 1 tablespoon orange juice, 1 teaspoon shoyu, 1 tablespoon spring water.

Mix 1 tablespoon tahini, 1 tablespoon brown rice vinegar, 1 teaspoon lemon juice, 1 teaspoon shoyu, 2 tablespoons spring water.

Things to Add to a Green Salad

- Lemon slices
- Toasted walnuts, almonds, or sunflower seeds
- Capers
- Cucumbers marinated in balsamic vinegar
- Grated apple
- Sliced grapes
- Crumbled tofu with a little umeboshi
- Arugula
- Can of drained beans
- Squares of deep fried tempeh or bread
- Radishes finely sliced and mixed with a little umeboshi vinegar

"Human beings, vegetables, or comic dust, we all dance to a mysterious tune, intoned in the distance by an invisible player."
—Albert Einstein

Exercise:
Sitting and eating together with friends and family will improve your health. Eating comfortably and slowly prevents overeating, and encourages relaxation, which aids digestion. The body processes food more effortlessly and efficiently when you are relaxed.

Take time to relish the scent, texture, and flavor of your food. Divide your meal into separate courses. Instead of bringing everything to the table at once, have a soup course, then a grain, bean and vegetable course, and finally dessert and tea. Take at least 5-10 minutes between each course to digest, chat, and relax. Whether you're dining with friends, family, or alone, set the table, sit down, and chill.

One Pot Cooking

Often we feel that we have little time to cook healthy foods. We fill our lives with so many activities that we forget to nourish ourselves. 'One Pot' Cooking is a great answer to those busy times and a fantastic way to put top quality fuel in our 'gas tank'. This style of cooking is considered to be one of the oldest and dates back many centuries. It has also been used throughout the world. One Pot Cooking is a quick and easy way to set hearty, satisfying meals on the table.

Another benefit to all-in-one cooking is that it saves time. It takes away some of the anxiety of trying to get many dishes finished at once. One pot cooking is a complete meal although a fresh salad or hot brown rice can add an extra dimension.

One-pot meals can vary from savory stews and spicy noodles to heartwarming skillet dinners. Plus, one-pot meals are a great way to use up leftovers, and the combinations are endless.

Think about the clean up! You don't have to wash every pot in the kitchen. Furthermore, many one-pot meals are not particularly 'sensitive', so you don't have to stand over them to make sure they cook 'on the dot'.

Most of the following all-in-one delicacies are made with a balance of whole grains, beans, vegetables, and some oil. Add an extra dish of calcium rich greens and you have a meal literally brimming with nutrition.

Menu:

- **Pleasing Pasta Stew**
- **Spicy Chinese Noodles**
- **Nabe**
- **Portuguese Naughty Rice**
- **Sukiyaki**
- **Tofu Mochi and Cabbage**
- **Bring It On Barley Stew**
- **3 Leftovers Cast off in a Stew**
- **Irish Seitan Stew**

Symbols for making the best recipe choice
S = Simple
A = Adventurous
V = Vegan
ST = Strengthening
R = Relaxing
C = Cleansing
E = Energizing

"Parsley—jewel of herbs, both in the pot and on the plate."
—Albert Stockli

Pleasing Pasta Stew

V S R

Here's an easy one dish meal that you can have ready to eat in under half an hour. If you use fresh herbs, this recipe takes a bit longer to make. Fresh herbs provide such an added zing of flavor that to experience is to believe!

Serves: 2 hungry people

Preparation and cooking time: 15 minutes

Ingredients:

1/2 can chickpeas
1/2 cup liquid from the can of chickpeas. Add extra water if needed
1/2 packet dry pasta (rotini or penne)
1 celery stalk, sliced thin on the diagonal
1 carrot cut in matchsticks
1/2 cup sliced green beans
1/4 cup chopped green or red pepper
1 tablespoon olive oil
1 tiny pinch cayenne
1 teaspoon fresh minced ginger
1/2 teaspoon dried basil OR 1 Tablespoon fresh minced
1/2 teaspoon dried thyme OR 1 teaspoon fresh minced
1/2 teaspoon dried marjoram OR 1 teaspoon fresh minced
4 tablespoons tomato puree
1 teaspoon salt or to taste
1/4 cup frozen peas
1 tablespoon chopped fresh parsley
1 teaspoon barley miso diluted in a little water
1 cup water
Ground black pepper optional
Soy cheese, optional

Utensils:

Large pot, pan with lid

Preparation:

Cook the pasta in boiling water for about 5 minutes. You want the pasta a little undercooked because it will cook again with the vegetables. Strain and rinse quickly.

Place the oil in a 4-6 quart pan and heat on medium.

Add the onion and sauté on a high flame for a minute. Add the carrot and continue to sauté for a minute. Repeat with the string beans, celery and pepper. Add the salt and mix through.

Add the herbs and spices, and sauté briefly.

Add the beans, water, and tomato puree. Bring to a boil and simmer for about 5 minutes.

Add the pasta to the veggies, and another cup of water. You can add more water for a soupier stew.

Add the minced parsley, frozen peas, and diluted miso

Cook for 3 more minutes

Serve in bowls, (with soy cheese and pepper on top if you like) and enjoy.

A large blanched vegetable salad works well with this dish or the *Cool Cucumber* recipe.

Tasty Tips

"Sauté" means to fry on med-high heat, stirring constantly. It's different from stir fry, which uses more heat, and is the end step in cooking. Usually after sautéing, the contents are subjected to another step, like steaming or adding to a soup or stew.

Examples of different tastes that can add a zing to your dishes:

Sweet - rice syrup, barley malt, mirin, carrot juice, carrots, onions, squash, parsnips, cabbage

Salty - miso, shoyu, sea salt, umeboshi, takuan pickle, shiso powder

Bitter - toasted nuts and seeds, mustard greens, broccoli rabe

Sour - lemon, brown rice vinegar, balsamic vinegar, umeboshi vinegar, dill pickles

Pungent - scallions, ginger, grated raw daikon, mustard, wasabi, chives

Spicy Chinese Noodles

SRE

Serves: 2 people

Preparation and cooking time: Various

Ingredients:
1 packet of udon noodles cooked as in the basic noodle recipe
1/2-1 tablespoon sesame oil
2-3 tablespoons shoyu
1 cup snow peas sliced
1 cup broccoli cut into small florets
1 cucumber diced
4 scallions finely sliced
2 tablespoons fresh parsley chopped
2 tablespoons balsamic vinegar
1 teaspoon mustard
Few drops hot sesame oil
Cooked shrimp for garnish (optional)

Utensils:
Large pan, medium pot with lid, bowl

Preparation:
Drain the noodles and rinse in cold water.
Whisk together the sesame oil and soy sauce, and toss with noodles.
Bring a pot of water t o a boil on a medium flame.
Turn the flame to high and add the broccoli.
Blanch for 2-3 minutes. Remove and place in a bowl.
Return the water to a boil and add the snow peas. Blanch for a minute.
Remove and place with the broccoli.
Add the cucumber, scallions and parsley.
Whisk the vinegar, mustard, and hot sesame oil, and toss this with the vegetables until well mixed.
Add the noodles and toss together until well combined.
Serve cold with a garnish of cooked shrimp.

Tasty Tips

Pre-cycle: Buy cloth or canvas bags for shopping instead of plastic and paper. Keep the bags in your car or hang on the back door as a reminder to take them to the store. If you do get paper or plastic bags, remember to recycle and return them to a health food store for re-use.

Nabe

Nabe means cooking pot and is a complete meal because it contains noodles, tofu, and vegetables. It is a relaxing and nourishing dish that helps you to feel eased after a busy day. Nabe is also good for circulation and is very warming.

VSR

Serves: 2-4 people

Preparation and cooking time: 20 minutes

Ingredients:
1 packet udon noodles lightly cooked for 1 minute and rinsed
1 bunch watercress rinsed and sliced
2 cups Chinese cabbage rinsed and sliced
1 carrot washed and finely sliced
2 shiitake rinsed and finely sliced
1 cup snow peas washed
1/2 block tofu cut into rectangles
1 inch piece kombu rinsed
6 cups spring water

Dipping Sauce:
2 tablespoons shoyu
2 tablespoons mirin
2 tablespoons brown rice vinegar
1/2 cup spring water
Shichimi 5 spice seasoning (optional)
Drop hot sesame oil (optional)
Garlic finely chopped (optional)

Utensils:
Traditional nabe pot or sturdy, deep pot with lid

Preparation:

Place the water and kombu in the pot and bring to a boil on a medium flame.

Remove the kombu and save it for use in another dish. Meanwhile, prepare the vegetables.

Arrange the vegetables (except for the watercress), noodles, and tofu attractively in sections around the pot.

Cover with a lid.

Bring to a boil on a high flame. As soon as it boils, turn off the flame, and add the watercress.

Mix the shoyu, mirin, vinegar, and water in a small bowl. This is the dipping sauce.

Serve from the Pot:

To serve, place a little dipping sauce in individual bowls. Add a selection of noodles, tofu, and vegetables, and pour the hot broth over the top. Garnish with a little 5 spice seasoning, garlic or hot sesame oil, if desired.

Note:

A great variety of vegetables can be used. Try winter squash, summer squash, daikon, cauliflower, pieces of fresh sweet corn, or string beans. The tofu can be deep-fried for a richer taste. Oysters or white fish can also be cooked in nabe.

Nutritious Nibbles

A few bowls of black and green olives, salty toasted nuts, raisins, dried apricots and apples, radishes sprinkled with sea salt, celery sticks filled with peanut butter, baby carrots with hummus, and slices of dill pickle are easy work for the chef, and make for yummy healthy appetizers, or movie watching snacks.

Portuguese Naughty Rice

In Portugal rice is one of the main grains. They often prepare it with a fish sauce or beans. This style of cooking rice is relaxing and nourishing. It helps bring your energy out to the surface and is at the same time substantial and satisfying.

S V ST R

Serves: 4 people

Preparation and cooking time: 50 minutes if you make the rice from scratch. Using leftover cooked rice it takes about 15 minutes.

Ingredients:
1 cup long grain brown rice rinsed
1 1/2 cups spring water
1 teaspoon sea salt
1 onion diced
1 carrot washed and grated
1 cup cabbage finely sliced
1/2 cup fresh or frozen peas
1 lead-free can chickpeas or beans of choice
1 bay leaf
1 clove garlic sliced (optional)
1 tablespoon olive oil
Sprig of cilantro for garnish

Utensils:
Large pan with lid, large skillet with lid

Preparation:
Place the rice, bay leaf, and water in a pan. Bring to a boil on a medium flame and add a pinch of sea salt.

Simmer, covered with a lid for about 45 minutes.

Meanwhile, warm the skillet over a high flame for a few seconds, and add the oil.

Add the garlic and onion to the oil and sauté for about 1 minute. Add the carrots and sauté a further minute. Repeat with the cabbage.

Add chickpeas and the rest of the salt.

Mix through the other vegetables.

Add 1/4 cup of water.

Place the cooked rice on top of the vegetables. Cook on a low flame, with a lid, for about 5 minutes.

Add the peas.

Mix the rice and vegetables together and serve from the skillet. Garnish with a sprig of cilantro.

*You can also use leftover rice or beans in this recipe. Simply add two cups of cooked rice after the vegetables have been sautéed and continue with the rest of the recipe. Leftover beans can be used instead of the chickpeas.

"The discovery of a new dish does more for the happiness of mankind than the discovery of a star."
—Anthelme Brillat-Savarin

Sukiyaki

S ST E - Vegan option included

This dish is an excellent way to get high energy that is long lasting. Sukiyaki is relaxing and helps your energy to flows more freely. It is nourishing and makes you feel less pressured. This is a great way to serve fish and is good for strengthening the blood.

Sukiyaki is a complete meal in itself and makes a great lunch or simple dinner. It can also be used as a side dish for a more elaborate meal. It is served from the skillet and everyone can gather around to serve themselves.

Serves: 2 people

Preparation and cooking time: 15 minutes

Ingredients:
1/2 pound white fish sliced
vegan option—use 1/2 block tofu sliced into squares
2 cups cooked udon noodles
1 carrot rinsed and finely sliced
2 cups Chinese cabbage rinsed and finely sliced
1 cup broccoli rinsed and cut into florets
1/2 cup string beans rinsed and halved
1/2-cup scallions rinsed sliced in half-inch pieces
1/2 cup spring water
1 tablespoon sesame oil
1 tablespoon shoyu
1 tablespoon mirin

Utensils:
Cast iron skillet with lid or heavy pot with lid

Preparation:
Warm the skillet on a medium flame for a few seconds.
Add the oil and warm for a few seconds.
Place the vegetables, fish and noodles in sections around the pot.

Add the water, shoyu and mirin. Cover with a lid and steam on a high flame for about 5 minutes.

Serve hot from the skillet.

To shallow fry the tofu, heat a small amount of sesame oil in a pan. When the oil is hot, add the squares of tofu. Cover with a lid and fry on a medium flame for about 3 minutes. Turn the tofu over and fry on the other side for 3 minutes more. Remove tofu and drain.

"Enjoying Sukiyaki"

Tofu Mochi and Cabbage

S V R

This dish is a huge favorite with my kids and their friends. A really quick and easy dish that leaves you satisfied and nourished; yet uplifted.

Serves: 2 people

Preparation and Cooking: 10 minutes

Ingredients:
1/2 block firm tofu crumbled
1/2 block mochi cut into rectangles or grated
1/2 head cabbage rinsed and shredded
2 tablespoons umeboshi vinegar mixed with the tofu
Few drops shoyu
1/2 cup spring water

Utensils:
Large skillet with lid

Preparation:
Place the water in a skillet.
Place the cabbage in the skillet.
Place the mashed tofu on top of the cabbage.
Place the mochi on top of tofu and sprinkle with shoyu.
Cover and steam on a high flame for about 7 minutes or until the mochi has melted.
This dish is served straight from the skillet.

Tasty Tips

When buying a cutting board, chose one made from bamboo. Bamboo is very strong and long lasting. Bamboo helps the eco-system as it is the fastest growing cover for re-greening, poor and degraded land, and actually cleans the air at the same time.

Bring It on Barley Stew

A V ST R

Barley is a light, uplifting grain that has a cooling effect on the body. Barley is a great grain for providing light, calming energy, and this dish is a marvelous stress reliever.

Serves: 4 people

Preparation and cooking time: 45 minutes
(most of this time is the stew simmering)

Ingredients:
1/2 cup hulled whole barley rinsed and soaked overnight
1/2 cup navy beans rinsed and soaked at least 3 hour or soaked overnight (these can be soaked with the barley)
1/2 onion cut into chunks
1 carrots cut into chunks
1 cup round cabbage rinsed and sliced
1 turnip cut into chunks
1 inch piece kombu
1 tablespoon miso diluted in a little water
1 tablespoon olive oil
2 cloves garlic sliced (optional)
1 cup broccoli rabe rinsed and sliced
Pinch sea salt
Spring water
Grated ginger for garnish

Utensils:
Pressure cooker, heavy pot

Preparation:
Layer the kombu, onion, cabbage, turnips, carrots, beans, and then the barley in a pressure cooker. Add enough water to cover the barley.
Cover with a lid and bring up to pressure on a medium flame.
Reduce the flame to medium/low and cook for 45 minutes.

Remove from heat and bring the pressure down.

Return to the heat and bring back to a boil.

Add the diluted miso and garlic and cook for about 3 minutes on a low flame.

Add the broccoli rabe and oil. Cook for another minute and serve garnished with grated ginger.

3 Leftovers Cast off in a Pot

A great way to use up leftovers, and gives you strong, grounded energy. A wonderful dish to enjoy before or after playing sports and physical activity.

Serve: 2-4 people

Preparation and cooking time: 15-20 minutes

Ingredients:

1 cup leftover grains
1 cup leftover beans
1 cup leftover vegetables
1 tablespoon brown rice miso diluted in a little water
2 cups spring water
1 teaspoon grated fresh ginger
1 slice of bread deep fried

Utensils:

Medium pot with lid

Preparation:

Place all the ingredients in a pot.
Bring to a boil on a medium flame.
Simmer on a low flame for 15-20 minutes.
For added richness add deep fried bread broken into small pieces.
Mix and serve with a garnish of ginger

Tasty Tips

Get to know your winter squash. To buy good squash, make sure the stem is really dried out, the color is deep and there is a patch of orange on the outside.

Acorn squash are deep green on the outside, orange inside and oval in shape. They are great for baking and are moist, rich and tender.

Buttercup squash are deep green with grey stripes and a pale green cup on the blossom end. The flesh is a bright orange. They are large and rounded with the top indented. These have the most marvelous sweet flavor and are great baked, in soups, purees or cooked with beans.

Butternut squash looks like a large peanut. It is pale orange on the outside and deep orange inside. Can be baked, steamed, cooked with beans or pureed.

Kabucha squash is a Japanese pumpkin and has a dull colored deep green skin with some pale green to white-colored stripes, and an intense yellow-orange color on the inside. The flavor is really sweet and they can be cooked in the same way as a buttercup squash.

Irish Seitan Stew

S V ST E

A great warming and stamina building stew. Perfect for the cold wintry weather.

Serves: 2-4 lovely people

Preparation and cooking time: 25 minutes

Ingredients:
1 cup seitan, diced
1 carrot roll-cut
1 parsnip roll-cut
1 onion diced
1 cup winter squash cut into chunks
1 inch piece of kombu
1 bay leaf
1/2 teaspoon dried rosemary (optional)
1 clove garlic, minced (optional)
1 teaspoon dried basil (optional)
1 teaspoon fresh parsley minced
1 bunch watercress sliced
1-2 cups water
1 tablespoon shoyu
1 tablespoon kuzu diluted in 4 tablespoons cold water
1-2 slices of deep fried bread (optional)

Utensils:
Medium pan with lid

Ingredients:
Layer the vegetables in the following order; Kombu, onion, squash, parsnip, carrot, and seitan.
Add enough water to cover the parsnips.
Cover and bring to a boil on a medium flame.

Add the herbs, garlic, and shoyu.
Simmer on a low flame for about 20 minutes.
Add the watercress and mix gently.
Add the diluted kuzu and mix through the stew until it thickens.
Serve with slices of deep fried bread or steaming hot brown rice.

> **"I feel a recipe is only a theme, which an intelligent
> cook can play each time with a variation."**
> **—Madam Benoit**

Exercise:
Grow herbs or sprouts on your window sill. There is something very uplifting about growing fresh greens in your kitchen. You can buy herbs already in pots and they only need a little watering now and again. Sprouts can be created from the seeds of radishes, broccoli, cress, kale, or daikon. Sprinkle a few seeds over a pot of soil and make sure to keep the soil damp. Enjoy the excitement of watching the bright green leaves burst forth. When they are a few inches high, snip the tender sprouts and use as a garnish for your favorite dish. Experience the alive and youthful energy they provide.

Dizzy Desserts

'Dinner is not dinner without dessert!' The first six dessert recipes are light and a great choice for weight control, and for feeling relaxed and uplifted. The rest are yummy, decadent, and worth making!

Menu:

- **Steamed Apples with Lemon**
- **Peach Surprise**
- **Appleberry Almond Sauce**
- **Kool Kanten**
- **Grill 'Em Pears**
- **Orange Mousse**
- **Scrumptious Oatmeal Cookies**
- **Ravishing Raspberry Torte**
- **Fresh Fruit Crumble**
- **Spicy Apple Cake**
- **Coffee Chocolate Chip Cake**
- **Peanut Brittle**
- **Chewy Crispy Crunch**
- **Ginger Snaps**
- **Beautilicious Brownies**
- **Chocolate Frosting**
- **Cashew Cream**
- **Whipped Tofu Topping**
- **Maple Cream Cheese Frosting**

"Stressed spelled backwards is desserts. Coincidence? I think not!"
—Author Unknown

Steamed Apples with Lemon

S V C R

This light and refreshing dessert helps the smooth function of the liver. Steamed apples provide a crisp, clean energy, and help take excess salt from the body.

Add a pinch of sea salt at the beginning of cooking and the fruit will be easier to digest and taste sweeter. Steamed apples are great way to satisfy sugar cravings.

Serves: 1 person

Preparation and cooking time: 7 minutes

Ingredients:
1 granny smith apple rinsed and sliced in eighths
1/2 teaspoon grated lemon rind
Pinch sea salt
1/2 cup apple juice

Utensils:
Medium pan with a lid

Preparation:
Place the ingredients in a pan.
Cover with a lid and bring to a boil on a high flame.
Cook the apples for 3 minutes.
Remove and serve warm.

Cleansing Menu
Basic Miso Soup
Basic Brown Rice
Nourishing Natto
Steamed Squash
Chinese Cabbage with Wakame
Steamed Apples with Lemon

Peach Surprise

S V R C

Serves: 4-6 people

Preparation and cooking time: 5-10 minutes

Ingredients:

4 peaches washed and sliced
1 cup vanilla rice milk
1 cup peach juice
1cup fresh raspberries washed
Pinch sea salt
3 tablespoons kuzu diluted in a little cold water
Mint for garnish

Utensils:

Medium pan

Preparation:

Place the peaches and raspberries in a bowl.
Place the rice milk and juice in a pan and heat on a medium flame.
When it begins to simmer, add the diluted kuzu and stir until thick.
Remove from the heat.
Mix gently and pour over the fruit.
Serve cool with a sprig of mint.

Appleberry Almond Sauce

SVRC

Serves: 4 people

Preparation and cooking time: 25 minutes

Ingredients:
4 apples washed, peeled and quartered
1 cup blueberries washed
2 tablespoons toasted almonds
1 teaspoon grated orange peel
Juice from an orange
1 cup apple juice
2 tablespoons rice syrup
Pinch sea salt

Utensils:
Medium pan with lid, blender

Preparation:
Place the apples, apple juice, orange rind, and sea salt in a pan.
Cover with a lid and bring to a boil on a medium flame.
Lower the flame and simmer for about 15 minutes.
Add the blueberries, rice syrup, and orange juice.
Mix through and remove from heat.
Place the nuts and a little juice from the apples into a blender.
Blend to a smooth cream.
Add the fruit and rest of the juice to the almond mixture.
Blend to a smooth creamy sauce.
Serve garnished with orange slices at room temperature or lightly chilled.

Kool Kanten

S V R C

Agar Agar flakes come from a sea vegetable and is the vegan version of gelatin. This dessert has a cooling effect on the body and is perfect for hot, summer weather or when you feel like chilling.

Serves: 6-8 people

Preparation and cooking time: 15 minutes

Ingredients:

4 cups strawberry juice
2 cups spring water
6 heaping tablespoons agar agar flakes
Pinch sea salt
1 cup raspberries rinsed
1 cup blueberries rinsed
1 cup strawberries rinsed and sliced
1 cup green grapes rinsed and halved

Utensils:

Medium pan, serving dish

Preparation:

Place the juice, water, salt and agar agar into a pan and heat gently on a medium, low flame.

Stir from time to time.

Place the fruit in a rinsed serving dish.

When the juice combination comes to a boil, stir and simmer for about 3 minutes.

Pour the hot liquid over the fruit.

Leave to cool and then place in a refrigerator to firm and chill.

Serve from the dish or cut and place in individual bowls.

Grill 'Em Pears!

S V R

An awesome way to cook fruit on the grill, simple, tasty, and fun. Inspired by my friend Patti Myers.

Serves: 1-2 people

Preparation and cooking time: 15 minutes

Ingredients:
1 pear cut in half with the center scooped out
Few blueberries
Rice syrup
Pinch sea salt

Utensils:

Aluminum foil

Preparation:
Place half a pear in the center of a square of foil.
Rub a few grains of sea salt over the pear,
Place some blueberries in the center.
Add a little rice syrup over the blueberries.
Wrap in the foil.
Place on the grill and cook for about 10 minutes.
Remove and enjoy.

"Grill 'Em Pears!"

Orange Mousse

S V R C

This dessert also uses agar agar flakes and is blended to create a wonderful creamy mousse, which is very soothing and calming
.

Serves: 4-6 people

Preparation and cooking time: 20 minutes

Ingredients:

2 cups almond amasake
2 cups apple juice
1 cup rice milk
6 tablespoons agar agar flakes
Pinch sea salt
1 teaspoon orange rind
1 cup juice from oranges
1 teaspoon vanilla essence
2-3 tablespoons rice syrup
Orange slices for garnish

Utensils:

Medium pan, blender

Preparation:

Place the amasake, juice, rice milk, agar flakes, sea salt and orange rind in a pan.

Bring to a boil on a medium/low flame.

Stir occasionally.

When the agar flakes are completely dissolved, remove from the flame and place in a dish to cool.

When the kanten is firm, blend in a blender with the orange juice, vanilla and rice syrup.

Serve garnished with orange slices. For a zesty alternative, use the juice from 3 lemons instead of the orange.

Scrumptious Oatmeal Cookies

S V

Serves: 8 people

Preparation and cooking time: 30 minutes

Ingredients:

1/2 cup safflower oil
1/2 cup rice syrup
1/2 cup maple syrup
1/2 cup tahini
1/2 cup apple juice
1/2 teaspoon sea salt
1 cup whole-wheat pastry flour
3 cups oatmeal
1 teaspoon cinnamon
1 cup raisins

Utensils:

Cookie sheets, blender, mixing bowl, cooling rack

Preparation:

Pre-heat the oven at 350 degrees. Oil the cookie sheets. Combine the first five ingredients in a blender and blend to a smooth consistency.

Place all the dry ingredients in a bowl and mix together. Gently add in the blended, wet ingredients.

Fold in the raisins. Let the batter sit for about 15 minutes.

Place a tablespoon, at a time, of the mixture on to the cookie sheets. Flatten gently. Bake for about 15 minutes or until golden brown.

Remove and let the cookies cool for 5 minutes before removing to a rack. Let cool completely before serving.

Tasty Tips

A little grated orange or lemon rind adds a sparkle to any cookie recipe.

Ravishing Raspberry Torte

S V

Serves: 8 people

Preparation and cooking time: 10 minutes/15-20 minutes baking

Ingredients:

1 cup almond flour
1 cup oat flour
1 cup whole-wheat pastry flour
1/4 cup chopped almonds
Pinch sea salt
1 teaspoon almond essence
1 teaspoon vanilla essence
1/2 cup safflower oil
1/2 cup maple syrup or rice syrup
Sugar free Jam

Utensils:

9 inch round pie dish, large bowl, blender, fork

Preparation:

Pre–heat the oven at 350 degrees.

Place the dry ingredients, almonds and salt in a large bowl and whisk lightly.

Place the oil, syrup, vanilla and almond essence into a small bowl. Whip together using a fork. Add the wet ingredients to the dry and mix gentle to form a crumbly dough. Try not to over mix.

Press two thirds of the dough into a 9 inch round pie dish. Spread a layer of raspberry jam over the top. Crumble a layer of the remaining dough over the top of the jam. Sprinkle with chopped almonds.

Bake in an oven for 15-20 minutes.

Idea:

A variety of different flavored jams can be used; apricot, strawberry, blueberry, or cherry.

Fresh Fruit Crumble

A V R

Serves: 8-10 people

Preparation and cooking time: 15 minutes/45 minutes baking

Ingredients:
1 1/2 cups whole-wheat flour
1/2 cup corn flour
1/2 cup chopped walnuts
1/2 teaspoon sea salt
1/3 cup safflower oil
1/3 cup maple syrup or rice syrup
1 teaspoon vanilla essence
2 teaspoons baking powder

Filling:
4 medium apples washed, peeled and sliced
4 peaches pits removed and sliced
2 cups raspberries rinsed
1 1/2 cups peach or apple juice
2 tablespoons kuzu diluted in a little cold water
Pinch sea salt

Utensils:
Baking dish, medium pan, small pan, mixing bowl

Preparation:
Preheat oven to 350 degrees. Place the apples, peaches, and raspberries in a baking dish. Put the juice and salt in a pan. Heat on a medium flame and add the kuzu.

Stir until thick. Pour over the fruit. Place the flours, baking powder, and salt into a large bowl.

Place the oil, vanilla, and sweetener in a bowl, and whip together with a fork. Add the wet ingredients to the dry ingredients.

Mix the ingredients together with your hands to form a crumble. Sprinkle over the fruit.

Cover with aluminum foil and bake in a medium oven for about 35 minutes. Remove cover and bake a further 5 minutes or until the crumble is golden and crispy.

Serve warm.

Spicy Apple Cake

A V R

This moist, spiced cake is easy to make and is a lovely, light version of traditional fruit cake

Makes: 12 servings

Preparation and cooking time: 10 minutes/45 minutes baking

Ingredients:

1/4 cup safflower oil
1/2 cup maple syrup or brown rice syrup
1/4 rice milk
1 teaspoon vanilla extract
1 cup unsweetened applesauce
1/2 cup raisins or 1/2 cup finely diced and peeled fresh apples
3/4 cup chopped walnuts
1 cup whole wheat pastry flour
1 cup unbleached white flour
2 teaspoons baking powder
1/2 teaspoon sea salt
1/2 teaspoon ground cinnamon
1/4 teaspoon mace
1/2 teaspoon powdered ginger
1/8 teaspoon ground cloves
Extra Apple Sauce

Utensils:
8 or 9 inch square baking pan, mixing bowl, small bowl

Preparation:
Preheat oven to 350°F.

Place the oil, maple syrup, rice milk, and vanilla into a small bowl, and whip together with a fork until smooth. Add the apple sauce and mix well.

Sift the flour, baking powder, sea salt, and spices into a mixing bowl. Whisk lightly.

Fold in the wet ingredients and mix lightly to form a dough. Fold in the raisins or apples and the walnuts.

The dough will be stiff.

Brush the baking pan with a little oil and add the dough.

Bake for 45 minutes, or until cake pulls away from edges of pan and a fork inserted in center comes out dry.

Cool on rack. Serve the cake with a generous spoonful of apple sauce or with the whipped tofu topping or cashew cream. Store in an airtight tin or container.

If the cake gets a little dry, refresh it by steaming in a steamer for a few minutes.

Tasty Tips

For a refreshing and heavenly treat, try frozen grapes. Simply rinse a small bunch of grapes and place them on a small cake pan. Freeze and enjoy the sorbet like flavor. You can pop them in a drink instead of an ice cube.

Coffee Chocolate Chip Cake

A V R

A spectacular cake to enjoy with friends over a cup of hot tea on a cold wintry afternoon.

Serves: 8-10 people

Preparation and baking time: 10 minutes/45 minutes baking

Ingredients:
1 1/2 cups whole-wheat pastry flour
2 cups unbleached white flour
1 1/2 cups grain coffee
2 tablespoons baking powder
1/2 teaspoon sea salt
1 cup apple juice
1 cup rice milk
1 cup safflower oil
1 cup maple syrup
1 tablespoon vanilla essence
3/4 cup chopped walnuts
1/4 cup semisweet vegan chocolate chips
1 teaspoon grated orange rind
Orange slices

Utensils:
Blender, mixing bowl, baking pan, strainer or sifter

Preparation:
Pre-heat the oven at 350 degrees. Sift the flours, baking powder, sea salt, and grain coffee into a mixing bowl and then whisk lightly with a hand whisk.

Place the juice, rice milk, oil, maple syrup, vanilla, and orange rind into a blender. Blend to a smooth cream.

Gently fold the wet ingredients into the dry ingredients to form a smooth batter. Add the chopped walnuts and chocolate chips, and mix and let sit for 5 minutes.

Brush a baking pan with oil. Pour the batter into the pan. Bake in the oven for about 45 minutes or until the cake shrinks away from the sides of the pan.

Test the middle by inserting a fork or chopstick. If it comes away clean and dry, the cake is ready.

Remove from the oven and cool before removing from the pan.

Serve with chocolate frosting, cashew cream or cream cheese topping, and decorate with orange slices, and toasted walnuts.

Tasty Tips

When making sugar and dairy free cakes, watch out for over mixing because the cake will turn out dense and heavy. Lightly fold the wet into the dry ingredients and mix gently until they are just blended to form a smooth batter.

Peanut Brittle

S V

Enjoy this great 'movie watching' snack.

Serves: 4-6 people

Preparation and cooking time: 15 minutes

Ingredients:
4 cups roasted unsalted peanuts
4-6 tablespoons barley malt or rice syrup
1 tablespoon maple syrup (optional)
1 teaspoon sea salt
1 tablespoon safflower oil
6-8 rice cakes finely crumbled

Utensils:
Small pan, baking dish or sheet, large bowl

Preparation:
Pre-heat the oven at 300 degrees.

Place the peanuts on a baking sheet and roast for 10 minutes.

Remove from the oven and place in a large bowl. Add the crumbled rice cakes.

Meanwhile, place the barley malt, maple syrup, oil, and salt in a pan. Bring to a boil on a medium flame. Simmer on a low flame until the syrup mixture starts to foam.

Pour the syrup over the peanuts and rice cakes, and mix through.

Place the peanuts back in the oven for five minutes. Mix thoroughly and continue to bake for a further 5minutes.

Remove and cool before serving. Turn the peanut brittle several times while cooling.

Chewy Crispy Crunch

S V

Another great snack for school, studying or to take on a picnic; very quick and easy to make.

Makes: about 12

Preparation: 5 minutes

Ingredients:
1/2 cup brown rice syrup
1/2 cup maple syrup
1/4 cup raisins (optional)
1/2 cup peanut butter*
4 cups sugar free crispy brown rice cereal
1/2 cup malt-sweetened vegan chocolate chips
Pinch sea salt

Utensils:
Medium pan, wooden spoon, square dish with sides, measuring cup, knife, serving dish

Preparation:
Place the rice syrup, maple syrup, sea salt, and peanut butter in a pan. Heat on a low flame and stir until creamy.
Add the chocolate chips and stir until melted. Remove from the heat.
Add the rice crispies and mix until coated. Lightly oil a square pan with a little safflower oil. Press the rice crispy mixture into the pan. Set aside to cool and firm. Cut into squares and serve.

* You can use other nut butters instead of the peanut butter. Try almond or hazelnut for a nutty treat. Use 1/2 cup peanuts instead of the peanut butter for a crunchier chew.

Ginger Snaps

S V

Makes: 18 cookies

Preparation and cooking time: 5minutes/12-15 baking

Ingredients:

3/4 cup oat flour
1/2 cup almond meal/flour
1/2 teaspoon baking powder
1/4 teaspoon sea salt
1 teaspoon ground ginger
1/2 teaspoon mace
1/4 cup safflower oil
1/4 cup rice syrup
1/4 cup maple syrup
1/2 teaspoon vanilla

Utensils:

Baking sheet, mixing bowl, small bowl, parchment paper

Preparation:

Pre-heat the oven at 325
Place the dry ingredients in a mixing bowl and lightly whisk.
Place the oil, vanilla and sweeteners in a small bowl and whip together with a fork.
Add the wet ingredients to the dry and mix gently to form a batter.
Cover 2 baking trays with parchment paper.
Place a tablespoon of cookie batter for each cookie on the sheets. Leave a good amount of space between each cookie because they spread. Makes about 18 cookies.
Bake in the oven for 15 minutes. These cookies cook quickly so you may want to check after 12 minutes.
Allow to cool before removing from the sheets.
Relish and enjoy!

Lemon Cookies can be made by switching the mace and ginger for one teaspoon natural lemon extract and one teaspoon lemon juice.

Beautilicious Brownies

S R

Makes: 12 Brownies

Cooking and preparation time: 10minutes/30 baking

Ingredients:
1 1/2 cups unbleached white flour
1/2 cup whole wheat pastry flour
1 cup maple syrup or brown rice syrup
3/4 cup unsweetened cocoa powder
1 teaspoon baking powder
1 teaspoon salt
1 cup sparkling water
1 cup safflower oil
1 teaspoon vanilla extract
1/2 cup semisweet vegan chocolate chips
1/3 cup chopped walnuts (optional)

Utensils:
9x13 baking pan, mixing bowl, small bowl

Preparation:
Preheat the oven to 350 degrees F (175 degrees C).

Sift the flours, cocoa powder, baking powder, and salt into a large bowl, and whisk lightly.

Place the oil, maple syrup, and vanilla in a bowl. Whip until well blended. Add the water and mix through.

Fold into the dry ingredients and mix gently until blended. Make sure not to over mix because it will result in a denser brownie.

Gently fold in chocolate chips (and walnuts if using).

Spread the batter evenly in a lightly oiled pan.

Bake for 25 to 30 minutes in the preheated oven, until the top is no longer shiny.

Cool for at least 10 minutes before cutting into squares.

Frostings and Toppings for Cakes, Pies and Puddings

Chocolate Frosting

S R

Makes: 2-3 cups

Preparation and cooking time: 5 minutes

Ingredients:

1 cup cocoa powder
1/2 cup maple syrup
1/2 cup tahini or almond butter
1 1/2 cups rice or almond milk
1/4 teaspoon sea salt
1 teaspoon almond extract

Utensils:

Blender, bowl

Preparation:

Place in a blender and blend to a smooth creamy frosting.
Add a little apple juice if the frosting is too thick.
Use as a topping for the Coffee Cream cake or with other pies and desserts

Cashew Cream

SVR

Serves: 6 people

Preparation and cooking time: 5 minutes

Ingredients:
2 cups unsalted roasted cashew nuts with the skins removed
1-1 1/2 cups apple juice
1-2 tablespoons tahini
2 tablespoons maple syrup
1 teaspoon lemon rind
1 tablespoon lemon juice
1 teaspoon vanilla extract

Utensils:

Blender, small pan

Preparation:
Place the apple juice, lemon and vanilla into a pot and warm on a low flame.

Place the cashews, maple syrup, tahini, and juice mixture in a blender, and blend to a smooth cream.

Use as a topping for the Coffee Cream cake or with other pies, and desserts.

Whipped Tofu Topping

S V

Although I am not a big advocate of using sweetened tofu, this is a delicious nondairy alternative to whipped cream. Keep blending until it is really creamy.

Serves: 1 cake

Preparation and cooking time: 5 minutes

Ingredients:
1 container silken tofu
1 tablespoon almond butter
2-3 tablespoons maple syrup
1 teaspoon vanilla or almond extract
1 tablespoon almond milk

Preparation:
Puree tofu, sweetener, almond butter, and vanilla or almond extract into a blender

Blend until very smooth and creamy. Add the almond milk if needed for a creamier texture. Chill for at least one hour before using.

It will firm slightly as it chills.

Makes about 1-2 cups.

Maple Cream Cheese Frosting

S R

This rich frosting is wonderful for special occasions. Use sparingly as it is rather rich.

Makes: Enough for 1 cake

Takes: 5 minutes

Ingredients:
8 ounces mock rice cream cheese
1/2 cup maple syrup
Juice of 1 lemon
1 teaspoon grated lemon rind

Preparation:
Cream all ingredients together until smooth.

"Once in a young lifetime one should be allowed to have as much sweetness as one can possibly want and hold."
—Judith Olney

Exercise:
Make a batch of Beautilicious Brownies. Find a cool container such as a colorful tin or decorate a small box. Tie it with a ribbon and give as a gift to a friend or family member.

Sip or Slurp

Menu:

Hot Apple Juice - uplifting and relaxing
Lemonade - stimulating
Fresh Fruity Punch - refreshing
Amaza-Shake - soothing
Oh So Smooth - really soothing
Bancha Twig Tea - balancing and cleansing
Barley Tea - cooling
Green Tea - cleansing
Grain Café au Rice Lait - naughty and satisfying
Ume So Kuzu Drink - strengthening
Ginger Lemon Cha - cleansing
Parsley Tea - uplifting and stimulating
Sweet Vegetable Tea - soothing and balancing
Carrot Daikon Drink - cleansing

Hot Apple Juice

SVRC

This simple drink is very relaxing especially if you have a hard time sleeping. It is good for relieving headaches that are deep inside or at the back of the head.

Serves: 1

Preparation and cooking time: 5 minutes

Ingredients:

1/2 cup apple juice
1/2 cup spring water
Slice of lemon (optional)

Utensils:

Small pan

Preparation:

Place the ingredients in a small pan. Heat on a medium flame until just boiling.
Remove and drink hot.

Lemonade

Serves: 4-6 People

Preparation and cooking time: 5 minutes

Ingredients:

4 cups apple juice
1/4 cup maple syrup
Juice of 4-6 lemons
Lemon slices and mint leaves for decoration

Utensils:

Jug, whisk

Preparation:

Place all the ingredients in a jug.
Whisk lightly with a whisk.
Serve chilled with slices of lemon and mint.

Tasty Tips

Pre-cycle plastic water bottles. Instead of recycling plastic water bottles, rinse them and use again. You can fill them with your own filtered water or buy a large container of spring water. Store the bottles in your fridge for later enjoyment.

Fruity Punch

S V

Serves: 4-6 People

Preparation and cooking time: 7 minutes

Ingredients:

1 bottle sparkling water
1 quart sugar free fruit juice such as grape, pear or strawberry
1 apple washed and sliced
1 cup raspberries rinsed
1 orange sliced
1 cup grapes rinsed and sliced in half
1 lemon sliced
Ice cubes

Utensils:

Jug

Preparation:

Place all the ingredients except for the sparkling water in a jug.
Mix gently and let sit for about 5 minutes.
Add the sparkling water just before serving.
Serve chilled.

Amaza-Shake!

S V R

Amasake is a creamy, rich, sweetener made from fermented rice. It is abundant in natural sugars as well as enzymes that aid with digestion and elimination. Amasake can be found in a drink form in most natural food stores. Use as a warm or cool drink or add to desserts. Amasake makes you feel more relaxed and calm and is very soothing and satisfying.

This 'all natural' smoothie tastes awesome and is great for your health. It is sugar and dairy free too!! A super quick drink/dessert for your family and friends. You can use rice milk instead of amasake in the smoothie if you prefer.

Serves: 3

Preparation and cooking time: 5 minutes

Ingredients:

1 cup almond amasake
1 cup rice milk
1 cup strawberry juice
1 cup strawberries washed and hulled
1 cup fresh peaches sliced
1 tablespoon maple syrup or rice syrup
Pinch sea salt
Strawberry slices for garnish

Utensils:

Blender, glasses

Preparation:

Place all the ingredients in the blender and blend to a smooth creamy texture. Serve chilled in individual glasses, garnished with strawberry slices.

Oh So Smooth

S V C

Serves: 2

Preparation and cooking time: 5 minutes

Ingredients:
1 banana
Juice of an orange
1 cup strawberries
1 cup blueberries
1 cup apple juice
1 cup rice milk
Pinch sea salt
1 tablespoon rice syrup or maple syrup

Utensils:
Blender

Preparation:
Place all the ingredients in a blender.
Blend to a smooth creamy texture.
Serve chilled with a garnish of strawberry.

Tasty Tips

Tea is the most commonly consumed beverage in the world after water. All tea contains polyphenols, which give it its antioxidant properties. Antioxidants help protect the body from free radical (oxidation) damage. Polyphenols also help to prevent blood clotting and lower cholesterol levels.

Bancha Twig Tea (Kukicha Tea)

S V R C

This is a great tea to drink on daily basis because it has an alkalizing effect on the blood, is strengthening, and calms the mind.

This mild, yet rich flavored tea comes from the leftover twigs of the tea bush. 'Originally known as 'peasants drink', the twigs are carefully selected and roasted to bring out their subtle flavor. Kukicha contains almost no caffeine. Caffeine is actually stored in the leaves of the tea bush.

Serves: 1

Preparation and cooking time: 5 minutes

Ingredients:

1 kukicha tea bag
1 cup boiling water

Utensils:

Pot or kettle

Preparation:

Place the tea bag in a cup.
Pour the hot water over the top.
Steep for 1-2 minutes.
Remove and save the tea bag for one more cup of tea.
Drink hot.

Option:

Add 1 teaspoon of rice syrup and a squeeze of lemon for a tangy flavor.

Tasty Tips

Energy moves in a spiral motion, constantly flowing from contraction to expansion and then back to contraction again. We can see this spiral of energy reflected in seashells, ferns as they unfold in the spring, or the way water disappears down a drain.

Barley Tea

S V R C

This tea has a cooling, relaxing effect on the body. Delicious when served chilled on a hot summers day.

Serves: 1

Preparation and cooking time: 5 minutes

Ingredients:

Barley tea bag
1 cup boiling water

Utensils:

Pot or kettle

Preparation:

Place the tea bag in a cup.
Pour the hot water over the top.
Steep for 1-2 minutes.
Remove and save the tea bag for one more cup of tea.
Drink hot or place in the fridge for a cool tea.

Green Tea

Green tea is the least processed of all leaf teas. The leaves are quickly steamed to give a light refreshing taste. This lovely tea is considered good for the heart, lowering cholesterol, immunity, and even preventing tooth decay! Watch out for drinking green tea late at night because it can keep you awake.

Serves: 1

Preparation and cooking time: 5 minutes

Ingredients:

Green tea bag
1 cup boiling water
Mint leaves (optional)

Utensils:

Pot or kettle

Preparation:

Place the tea bag in a cup.
Pour the hot water over the top.
Dip a mint leaf into the tea and swirl around for an added hint of freshness.
Steep for 1-2 minutes.
Remove and discard the tea bag.
Drink hot or place in the fridge for a cool tea.

From The Beatles "All Too Much"
"Sail me on a silver sun
Where I know that I'm free
Show me that I'm everywhere
And get me home for tea"

Grain Café au Rice Lait

SVR

Makes: one serving.

Takes: 5 minutes to make

Ingredients:
1 cup rice or almond milk
1 tablespoon grain coffee (instant grain coffee powder)
Sprinkle of cinnamon
1 teaspoon rice syrup

Utensils:
Small pan

Preparation:
Place the grain coffee into a large mug.

Place the rice or almond milk in a small pan and bring to boil on a medium flame

Pour the hot rice or almond milk over the grain coffee and stir. If desired, add a sprinkle of cinnamon and a teaspoon of rice syrup. Sip and enjoy.

Ume Sho Kuzu

S V ST C

This drink is a great way to build immunity and to help prevent colds and flu. It strengthens the digestion and restores vitality. If you add a little fresh ginger juice, the drink will improve circulation and warm the body.

Have the drink three days in a row if you feel a cold coming or enjoy 1-2 times a month for prevention.

Serves: 1

Preparation and cooking time: 7 minutes

Ingredients:
1 heaping teaspoon kuzu (powder from the kuzu plant)
1/2 to 1 umeboshi plum (Japanese sour plum that is pickled in salt)
1 cup cold water
Several drops to 1/2 teaspoon shoyu
Optional: 1/2 teaspoon fresh ginger juice

Utensils:

Small pan

Preparation:
Dissolve the kuzu in a cup of cold water.
Mix well to make sure it is completely dissolved.
Place the kuzu in a small pan.
Heat on a medium flame and stir constantly. The liquid will become a transparent gelatin. Bring to a boil.
Break the umeboshi into small pieces and add to the kuzu.
Add the shoyu and mix gently. Add the ginger if desired.
Stir through and remove from the heat. Drink while hot.

Parsley Tea

SVC

This tea is uplifting and stimulating and gives the brain an energy boost.

Serves: 1

Preparation and cooking time: 7 minutes

Ingredients:
1/2 cup parsley rinsed and finely chopped.
2 cups water

Preparation:
Bring the water to a boil. Add the parsley and simmer, covered for about 5 minutes.
Strain and drink hot.

Ginger Lemon Cha

S V C

A wonderfully, stimulating tea that helps to open up your energy and thinking.

Serves: one serving.

Takes: 5 minutes to make

Ingredients:

Juice of 1/2 lemon
1 teaspoon fresh ginger juice.
1 cup boiling water

Preparation:

Place the juice of half a lemon and the ginger juice in a cup.
Add the hot water and a few slices of lemon for an invigorating tea.
Drink hot.

"If you are cold, tea will warm you. If you are too heated, it will cool you. If you are depressed, it will cheer you. If you are excited, it will calm you."
—Gladstone, 1865

Sweet Vegetable Tea

S V R C

This tea helps to balance blood sugar and prevent the highs and lows of energy during the day. It is very relaxing and when taken daily, prevents sweet cravings.

Cut extra vegetables so you can make it easily the following day. This tea is best made fresh everyday.

Serves: 2-3

Preparation and cooking time: 25 minutes

Ingredients:
1/4 cup onion finely sliced
1/2 cup carrot finely sliced
1/2 cup cabbage finely sliced
1/2 cup winter squash finely sliced
4 cups spring water

Utensils:
Medium pan with lid, vegetable skimmer

Preparation:
Bring the water to a boil.
Add the vegetables and return to a boil.
Cover and simmer for about 15-20 minutes.
Strain the vegetables immediately and drink the liquid only.

Tasty Tips

The finer you grate carrots, the sweeter the flavor.

Carrot and Daikon Drink

S V R C

This drink is very cleansing and helps with weight loss and to dissolve hardened fat in the body. Enjoy for a few days in a row.

Serves: 1 person

Preparation and cooking time: 5 minutes

Ingredients:
1 heaping tablespoon finely grated carrot
1 heaping tablespoon finely grated daikon or radish
1/2 umeboshi plum
1/2 sheet toasted nori torn into little pieces
Squeeze of lemon
Drop shoyu
1 cup spring water

Utensils:
Small pan

Preparation:
Place the carrot, daikon, umeboshi, nori, and water in a pan.
Bring to a boil on a medium flame.
Simmer on a low flame for 3 minutes.
Add a drop of shoyu and a squeeze of lemon.
Drink hot.

Exercise:
Practice portion control. Try to stop eating when you are about 80% full. To embrace the idea, eat slowly, take small mouthfuls, and chew well. Put down your fork and remove your plate at the first twinge of fullness rather than taking a break and eating more. Use smaller plates and bowls when setting the table and opt for having more vegetables. If you still feel a little peckish, finish your meal with a nice big cup of hot tea.

The Natural Medicine Cabinet

There is something deeply nurturing about healing the self.
The following remedies are simple, effective and can be made at home.
They are inexpensive and easy to prepare.

Headaches at the Back of the Head or Deep Inside

- Hot apple juice. A little lemon juice can be added if desired.
- Steamed leafy greens, parsley tea.

Sides of the Head at the Temples

- 1 tablespoon grated daikon radish in 1 cup hot kukicha tea with a drop of shoyu.
- Steamed cabbage with sauerkraut.

Front of Head or After Eating Sugar

- 1 umeboshi plum.
- 1 teaspoon of shoyu in a cup of hot kukicha tea.
- Miso soup is also helpful for this kind of headache.

In General for All Headaches

- Soak feet in warm water for 10 minutes.
- Massage the hands and feet.

Insect Bites and Bee Stings

- Slice a piece of daikon, onion or scallion and rub it over the bite.
- Lavender and peppermint essential oils are good for bites and stings.
- Lemongrass, lemon, peppermint, and lavender essential oils keep the bugs away!
- Green clay mixed to a paste with a little water is great for bee stings or any insect bites.
- Moistened tobacco is wonderful for bee stings.

Menstrual Cramps

Suggestions:

- A week before your period is due cut back on salty, oily, baked foods like chips, French fries, cookies, crackers, chocolate, nut butters, or refined flour.
- Eat less fish and watch your intake of salt.
- If you have cramps when your period starts, make a drink from 1 teaspoon kuzu powder diluted in a cup of cold water. Cook on a medium flame until liquid becomes clear. Add 1 teaspoon of shoyu and drink hot.
- Place a hot water bottle on the belly.
- Massage the feet.
- Regular exercise such as walking helps to regulate the menstrual cycle.
- Use ginger in cooking to help with nausea and bloating.

Remedy for Colds and Flu

- Ume Sho Kuzu - This drink is a great way to build immunity and to help prevent colds and flu. It strengthens the digestion, and restores vitality. If you add a little fresh ginger juice before serving, the drink will improve circulation and warm the body. Have the drink three days in a row if you feel a cold coming or enjoy 1-2 times a month for prevention.
- Miso soup with some fresh ginger added at the end.
- Soft rice cooked with umeboshi. This gruel is nourishing, soothing, and easy to digest.
- Soak feet in hot water with a few tablespoons salt added for about 10 minutes.
- Place a hot towel on the shoulders.

"Remedy for Colds and Flu"

Constipation

It is normal to sometimes become constipated when adjusting to a grain based diet.

Suggestions:
- Increase the proportion of fresh vegetables.
- Gently massage the belly in a clockwise direction, pressing firmly around the outside for 3 circles, and then around the belly button in 3 circles.
- Soak feet in hot water.
- Drink kanten tea for 3 days in a row.
- Increase beans and serve with a little grated radish or ginger.
- Try to walk for 30 minutes a day.

Remedy for Constipation:
Kanten Tea
This is a simple tea that helps to relax and regulate the digestion.

Ingredients:
1 cup spring water
1 tablespoon agar agar flakes
1 tablespoon rice syrup or barley (optional)

Preparation:
Place the agar agar flakes and cold water in a pan.
Bring to a boil on a medium flame.
Simmer for about 5 minutes, stirring constantly until the flakes are dissolved.
Add a tablespoon of rice syrup or barley malt.
Remove from heat. Drink warm.

Sore Throat

Gargle with 1 cup of room temperature kukicha tea and 1/2 teaspoon sea salt.

Sip on hot kukicha tea with a tablespoon of rice syrup and a squeeze of lemon.

Tasty Tips

Finely grated apple or hot apple juice can help to reduce a mild fever

Bloating

- Increase intake of sweet vegetables especially carrots, parsnips, onions, and squash.
- Drink a few cups of carrot juice a week.
- Cut back on flour products.
- Change from whole wheat to spelt bread.
- Watch your intake of salt and dry foods like crackers, chips, or rice cakes.
- Choose roasted nuts if you crave a crunchy taste.
- Have 1 tablespoon of grated daikon or red radish with your meals.

Skin Problems

Suggestions:

- Increase the proportion of fresh vegetables especially dark green leafy like kale, collards, and watercress.
- Drink carrot juice, water and herbal teas.
- Avoid eating chocolate, fried foods, and refined sugar especially sodas.

Try one of these remedies for a while before switching to another.

- The cooling gel from Aloe Vera plant is a highly effective natural cure against Acne. This enzyme-rich gel has very soothing anti-inflammatory, and anti-bacterial properties.
- Tea tree oil is very effective as it contains bacteria-fighting substances called Terpenes. Acne is often caused by bacteria and the Terpenes destroy or weaken them enough to be cleared up by protective antibodies.
- Dab a small amount of toothpaste (paste, not gel) on pimples before bed and rinse off in the morning. The paste helps to dry out the pimples.
- Apply fresh lemon juice on the affected area overnight. Wash off with warm water the next morning.
- A rather unusual remedy is to rub fresh garlic over the acne or pimples. Stinky but effective!

Minor Burns and Sunburn

Suggestions: Try one!

- Put toothpaste over the burn. Leave it overnight and then rinse it off in the morning. Takes away the pain and doesn't leave a scar.
- Cut a slice of tomato and rub it over the burn. The acid from the tomato takes the pain away and the burn doesn't blister.
- The aloe vera plant is excellent for burns. Just break a piece off the plant and rub the burn with the gel that comes from inside. You can also use the pure aloe vera gel. This is also very good for sunburn.
- Pour white vinegar over the burn. It helps to disperse the heat and takes away the pain. Great for sunburn too.

Special Suggestions

Salt baths can improve the way you feel and ease away tension. Good for aches and pains, tired feet, and stiff or sore muscles. Adding a little salt to your water can actually help improve your circulation, purify the skin, and help you to feel more positive. Use a small handful of sea salt to a bath full of water. Combine with essential oils like lavender or orange for extra relaxation.

A hot water bottle is an awesome warmer for cold, wintry nights. It can warm up your bed, and your toes; helping you to relax and sleep well. A hot water bottle is wonderful for aches and pains, muscle tension, flu, or menstrual cramps. It is cheap and easy to use.

Uva Ursi is a marvelous herbal tea for treating urinary tract infections. Also known as bearberry, this herb has a history of medicinal use dating back to the 2nd century. Native Americans also used it as a natural antibiotic and remedy for bladder and related infections.

Healthy Steps to Your Ideal Weight

Many teenagers and students worry about losing or gaining weight. Here are some suggestions to help you maintain your natural weight.

To lose weight:

- Replace refined carbohydrates like bread, cookies, sweets, peanut butter, or fried and fatty foods with fruits, nuts, vegetables, whole grains, and beans.

- Eat a larger portion of vegetables; about 50% of daily intake. Vary the cooking styles.

- Have a large bowl of vegetable soup every day.

- Include daikon and radishes on a regular basis. You can finely grate a tablespoon of daikon, or radish and have it as a condiment with rice. These vegetables help to break down fat and discharge it from the body.

- Focus on eating whole grains; brown rice, barley, millet, and whole oats rather than cracked grains, and breads. Choose recipes in the book with the cleansing symbol C.

- Eat a small portion of rinsed sauerkraut or light pickles on a daily basis.

- Cut back on salty foods and salt in general.

- Eat slightly more, lightly cooked vegetable dishes, than the heavy, rich ones.

- Use olive oil and sesame oil in cooking rather than having nut butters, or rich salad dressings. If a recipe calls for oil, use half the recommended amount or replace with 1 tablespoon of water.

- Take the carrot daikon drink every day for a week and then 2 times a week for a month.

- Have a sheet of toasted nori everyday. The minerals in nori help to break down excess fat in the body.

- Eat a comfortable amount but take one portion of each dish and don't go back for seconds

- Standing up to eat and picking at food are major contributors to weight gain. Break these habits by sitting down to eat everything even the smallest morsel.

- Serve all your foods from bowls or plates. Eating out of bags or containers makes it easier to eat more. Refrain from watching TV, or reading while eating. This encourages over eating because you are not as conscious of how much you are putting in your mouth.

- Choose to focus on your overall health and wellbeing, and not your weight. When we put our attention to something, it tends to show up. It is much easier to naturally lose those extra pounds when you are happy and busy doing the things you love.

- If your diet already seems healthy, try to get more exercise such as walking, cycling, running in nature, or daily stretching and yoga. Find things to do that make you really feel joyful or start a new hobby.

To gain weight:

- It is important to have a wide variety of different foods and tastes. Use mustard, olive and sesame oil, nut butters, vinegars, lemon, grain syrups, a little spice, and ginger in cooking.

- Include slightly more oil, nuts, seeds, mochi, beans, tofu, or tempeh into your diet on a regular basis.

- Make sure to have a variety of well cooked, nourishing dishes; as well as lightly cooked vegetable dishes.

- Use a variety of whole grains, pasta, cracked grains, and refreshed bread.

- It is more important to focus on eating a variety of tastes and ingredients rather than trying to eat larger portions.

- Include some gentle exercise such as walking, yoga, or stretching. Find ways to relax such as reading, listening to inspiring music, meditation, gardening, or being in nature.

For both gaining and losing weight:

- Cut back on salty dishes and salt in general.

- Sit down to eat all food even snacks.

- Eat regular meals at the same time each day.

- Eat slowly and chew well.

- Stop eating at least 2 hours before bed.

- Have plenty of healthy snacks (carrot and celery sticks, miso ramen noodles, applesauce, berries, cucumbers) handy in case you need something in a hurry.

- Make sure to eat three or more times a day whether you are trying to gain weight or lose weight. It is hard to get all of the nutritious foods and energy you need if you only eat one meal a day.

- Do the hot towel rub everyday.

- If you feel that you cannot control your eating behavior or if you are losing a great deal of weight, you should discuss this with a qualified practitioner

The Hot Towel Rub

This is especially good for beautiful skin, weight control, stress relief, and low energy.

This simple routine is a lovely, inexpensive way to get beautiful, glowing skin. All you need is a cotton face cloth and a sink full of hot water. The idea is too stimulate and cleanse the skin by rubbing briskly with a hot, damp towel. This is different from using a loofa because a hot towel rub also stimulates the muscles beneath the skin.

Healthy skin is smooth, soft to the touch, gently moist, and firm but not tight. It looks fresh and radiant and is a reflection of our overall health.

Our skin is the largest organ in the body; it renews itself every 28 days. The cells go through a continuous cycle of death and renewal, and in a healthy or an unhealthy manner depending on our lifestyle. Most of us try to keep our skin fresh and youthful with costly creams and remedies that only serve to clog the surface. A healthy diet is the most important factor in having beautiful skin, although a hot towel rub will nourish it on a daily basis.

The skin is the barrier between our inner and outer worlds. It protects us from the environment, affects how we respond to heat and cold and literally holds us together. Healthy skin helps us to develop sensitivity to pressure and touch and also strengthens our immune system.

The biggest problem that most people have is clogged skin. As a result, toxins, which are normally released through the skin, are reabsorbed into the body. When our skin is healthy, we release tension, stress and pressure easily and feel comfortable with who we are. If our skin is clogged then it is difficult to let go of pressure and feel relaxed or good about ourselves.

Dry skin is the result of clogged pores so moisture and oil cannot easily pass through. This is most commonly caused by a high fat diet. Using moisturizers that are high in mineral, coconut, or palm oil make the matter worse by coating the surface.

The hot towel rub also takes the strain off the kidneys, liver, and intestines. These organs are also responsible for discharging toxins. When they overwork, the toxins cannot be smoothly eliminated and move to the surface in an attempt to exit, resulting in rashes, pimples, or other skin irritations. When we rub our body all over, we stimulate the meridians in the body thus increasing the energy that is sent to the internal organs. Meridians are streams of energy that connect to the organs. They nourish the organs and help them to discharge. Therefore, the hot towel rub also stimulates our organs and helps them to rest, repair, and function well.

The hot towel rub improves circulation and strengthens the immune system. It is a great stress reliever. If you do the rub in the morning, you will feel uplifted and ready for the day. At night, the rub helps you to feel relaxed and sleep more soundly. In general, it will help you to detoxify, let out tension, lose weight, improve energy, and strengthen your health.

The Easy Routine

All you need is a top quality, ideally organic, cotton face cloth (not too soft), a sink full of hot water, and your bathroom. You can add a few drops of essential oil like lavender or peppermint to your water for added relaxation or stimulation.

1. Fill your bathroom sink with hot water.
2. Dip the face cloth into the water, wring it out, and fold it into a pad that fits comfortably in your hand.
3. Rub your entire body in a back and forth motion. The strokes should be short and fairly brisk. The idea is to have your skin turn pink. You do not need to rub really hard; the pressure should be firm but not painful. Watch for areas that are delicate or sensitive and be gentle. This includes the area along the spine and face.
4. Dip your face cloth in the hot water from time to time to refresh it. Change the water periodically. You will be amazed at how dirty it becomes!
5. Sometimes, areas of your skin may get a little dry or fail to turn pink at all. Don't give up at this point. When fat builds up below the surface of the skin, it prevents the natural oils from flowing smoothly. As the fat breaks down, your skin will become smooth and silky to the touch. You might also feel

angry or not like to rub certain parts of your body. Work gently through this resistance by breathing into the specific area and spending a little more time there. This will help you feel more open and loving towards your body and develop a better self-image.

6. Pay special attention to your hands, feet, face, and groin area. If you are too busy to do the full rub, just concentrate on these areas.

7. Keep the rub separate from the bath or shower. You tend to lose minerals if you are standing or sitting in water for a long time.

8.If you can't resist using a moisturizer, it is better to apply it before bed rather than in the morning. Be sure to choose one that is made with natural vegetable oils such as sesame, olive, or sunflower, is paraben-free, and hasn't been tested on animals.

9. The hot towel rub can be done in the morning or at night or both. The routine usually takes between 10 to 15 minutes and feels like a mini workout too!

Special Dishes for Specific Situations

Special Dishes that can be included into your daily diet for:

Playing sports - soba noodles in broth, fried bread added to bean dishes, long sautéed dishes, nori rice balls, fish dishes, add burdock root to bean and vegetable dishes, increase vegetable protein, fried rice balls.

Stress relief - Soothing sweet veggie soup, millet crush, smashing squash and sweet potato, blanched vegetables, tofu mochi cabbage, nabe, udon noodles in broth, barley stew, cool cucumbers, carrot juice, hot apple juice.

Concentration - nori rice balls, pressure cooked brown rice, Chinese cabbage with wakame, basic miso soup, hearty steamed vegetables, sauerkraut and takuan pickles, steamed granny smith apples, lemon ginger cha.

Increased energy - Irish seitan stew, barley stew, deep fried rice balls, noodles in broth, Chinese cabbage and wakame, sukiyaki, ume sho kuzu drink, hearty steamed vegetables.

Making Menus

Spring
Luscious Lemon Broth
Portuguese Rice
Vegetable Medley
Cool Cucumbers
Appleberry Almond Sauce

Summer
Cool Lettuce and Pea Soup
Mediterranean Noodle Salad
Simple Steamed Carrots
Watercress Apple Rolls
Orange Mousse

Fall
Lovely Lentil Soup
Millet Crush
Sweet Daikon
Garden Salad with Creamy Tofu Dressing
Fresh Fruit Crumble

Winter
Vital Veggie Soup
Deep Fried Rice Balls
Bountiful Baked Beans
Mixed Greens with Tangerine
Spicy Apple Cake

Quick Dinners for Seven Days

Day 1
Noodles, Beans, and Miso soup
Pan Fried Mochi
Minted Carrot and Peas
Watercress Apple Rolls

Day 2
Barley Stew
Stuffed cucumbers

Day 3
Garlic Rice
Ginger Shoyu Tofu
Hearty Steamed Vegetables
Simple Blanched Greens

Day 4
Soothing Sweet Veggie Soup
Tofu Pasta Sauté
Blanched Greens, Carrots, and Cabbage

Day 5
Couscous Pilaf
Sweet and Sour Seitan
Steamed Greens

Day 6
Pressure Cooked Brown Rice and Barley
Unchillin Chili
Blanched Peas and Cauliflower

Day 7
English Onion Soup!
Rice Balls
Scrambled Tofu
Steamed Greens and Corn (off the cob)

General Guidelines for Daily Eating

Breakfasts Ideas
Make enough soft cereal for 2 days
Oatmeal
Softly rice
Golden Grits - make enough to fry the next day
Fried Polenta
Refreshed Bread
Orange Walnut Pancakes
Pan Fried Mochi

Make Enough Vegetables for Lunch
Simple Blanched Vegetables
Simple Steamed Vegetables
Sauerkraut

Lunch Ideas
Tofu Mochi Cabbage
Sukiyaki
Soba or Udon in Broth
Any sandwich, wrap, or pita with fillings from "Between the Slices"
Rice balls
Sushi
Corn on the Cob with Umeboshi
Any leftover grain, vegetable, or bean dishes from dinner
Vegetables cooked at breakfast

Dinner Ideas
Choose 1 soup,
Choose 1 dish from grain
1 dish from long cooking
1 dish from short cooking.
Long cooking dishes include beans.
Short cooking dishes include tofu and natto.
Dessert is optional

Examples of Soups
Luscious Lemon Broth
Basic Miso Soup
Lovely Lentil Soup
Cool Lettuce and Pea Soup
Soothing Sweet Veggie Soup
Fab Fish Soup
Nabe

Examples of Grains
Pressure Cooked or Boiled Brown Rice
Millet Mash
Barley Stew
Couscous Pilaf
Tofu Pasta Sauté
Walnut Pesto Pasta
Mediterranean Noodle Salad
Any of the lunch grain suggestions

Examples of Protein Dishes
Unchillin Chili
Bountiful Baked Beans
Ginger Shoyu Tofu
Tofu and Veggie Stir Fry
Sweet and Sour Seitan
Nutritious Natto
Tomato Basil Salmon

Examples of Long Cooking
Steamed Vegetables
Irish Seitan Stew
Hearty Steamed Vegetables
Vegetable Medley
Squash and Sweet Potato Mash
Sweet Daikon
Hiziki with Peanut Butter

Examples of Short cooking
Blanched Vegetables
Garlic Broccoli
Chinese Cabbage with Wakame
Mixed Greens with Tangerine
Watercress Apple Rolls
Cool Cucumbers
Garden Salad with Creamy Tofu Dressing

Examples of Desserts
Steamed Apples with Lemon
Peach Surprise
Appleberry Almond Sauce
Amazashake
Ravishing Raspberry Torte
Fresh Fruit Crumble
Chewy Crispy Crunch

Examples of Teas
Green tea
Bancha twig
Hot apple juice
Sweet veg tea
Carrot daikon drink
Carrot juice
Barley Tea
Grain Café au Rice Lait

Extras:
1 sheet toasted nori with grains or in soup
Shiso powder on grains
Toasted seeds and nuts
Sauerkraut
Dill Pickles
Takuan Pickle

Cool Stuff for Natural College Life

Aroma Help

The ancient art of Aromatherapy dates back to Egyptians in 3000 BC and has since been used throughout the world as a way to sooth and heal the body. Aromatherapy uses essential oils from plants, flowers, and seeds, each with their special fragrance and unique effect on the emotions, mind and physical body.

Easy ways to use Essential Oils:
Add a few drops to a bath for deep relaxation.

Mix a few drops with a little almond oil and massage into the body, hands, or feet. It is best to keep out of the sun after putting essential oils on the skin. Place a few drops on a warm, damp washcloth and use in the shower, or hold over face.

Add a few drops to a handkerchief and place it near your pillow, or in your school or travel bag.

Useful Essential Oils:
Bergamot, Peppermint, Lavender, Orange, Lemon, Geranium

Their Benefits:
(Mix them together for a unique blend of smells and beneficial effect.)

Alertness
Bergamot, peppermint

Mental Stimulation
Lemon, peppermint

De-Stress
Bergamot, orange, geranium

Improve Sleep
Orange, lavender

Confidence
Orange

Lift Spirits
Peppermint, bergamot, geranium

Contentment
Lavender, bergamot, orange

Creativity
Bergamot, lemon

Focus
Lemon, bergamot, peppermint

Happiness
Orange, geranium

Joy
Lemon, orange, bergamot

Peace
Lavender

Concentration and performance
Bergamot, lemon, lavender

Positive Feelings
Lemon, geranium

Restfulness
Lavender, geranium

Self-esteem
Geranium

Self-image
Orange, lavender

Skin Irritations and Redness
Peppermint. lavender

Headaches
Lemon, peppermint, lavender

Tasty Tips

Bring lovely scents into your home, or room with fragrant flowers, bowls of natural pot pourri, or shake a few drops of essential oil onto a light bulb. Place apple juice and a stick of cinnamon in a pan, and simmer. Enjoy the warming fragrance that drifts throughout.

Remember to use green cleaners, natural fragrances, and organic, paraben free beauty products.

Simple Feng Shui for Dorm Rooms

Feng shui is the ancient art of placement and is very effective for helping you to feel more at home in your room.

Ideas:

Place a living plant next to your computer. Plants create a fresh and alive atmosphere, and bring in radiant energy. Plants also help to balance the electromagnetic radiation that comes off computers, which can make you feel drained, or tired. Plants with rounded leaves are more calming, and best suited to smaller rooms.

Hang a multi-faceted crystal in the window. Crystals bring in energy from the sun in the form of patterns of light that dance on the walls. Crystals are very good at brightening a dark, or stagnant room.

Rock Salt Crystal Lamps are natural air ionizers, and add a soft, relaxing orange glow to your room. Hand crafted from the foothills of the Himalayas, these lamps add healthy negative ions, and help you to feel refreshed, uplifted, and peaceful.

Choose a good direction for studying and working on the computer. If you have a laptop, it is a more versatile and easier to move to a beneficial direction. Look to see where the sun rises which is in the east. If you sit facing east or in the eastern part of the room, you will feel more active, motivated for a quick start, and able to get your work done. Sitting in the north west and facing south east helps you to feel more in control of your life, develop organizational skills, and plan ahead. Sitting in the west creates feelings of romance and contentment, and is good for socializing.

Colors can be used to create a mood in a room. Pastel colors like blue and green have a cooling and relaxing effect whereas bright colors such as reds and oranges are warm and stimulating. Yellows and creams are more balanced. Pale colors are most suited for restful sleep, and feeling calm. Bold colors are great when used as accents in cushions, posters, or bedding.

Use natural cotton, wool, or silk next to your skin or for your bedding. Cotton has less static electrical charge than other material. When worn next to the skin, cotton helps to neutralize imbalances in the body. Synthetics on the other hand, increase imbalances. So if you are feeling more tired, or anxious, synthetics will actually make you feel worse.

Exercise:
Start a list of all the blessings you have in your life. Add to it on a daily basis. Blessings don't have to be big things...a smile from a friend, watching a beautiful hummingbird flutter around a flower, laughing with your sisters, or maybe listening to a great song. Positive, happy memories 'up' your vibrations and raise your spirit. If you focus on the good things in your life, then many more exquisite experiences will come your way.

"Eat Me Now"

Some Useful Websites

www.celebrate4health.com - Melanie's site
www.chienergy.co.uk
www.macrobiotics.co.uk
www.llusciousorganic.co.uk
www.michaelrossoff.com
www.strengtheninghealth.org
www.macroamerica.com
www.kushiinstitute.com
www.e-macrobiotica.com
www.cybermacro.com
www.fortunateblessings.org
www.hipchicksmacrobiotics.com
www.christinacooks.com
www.mecidart.com - Megan's art

Melanie provides individual and family way of life counseling, macrobiotic cooking classes, feng shui consultations, and full day seminars. The counseling sessions can be in person, by phone, or email. Melanie offers full support in getting started with macrobiotics.

Email: info@celebrate4health.comPhone: 610 594 6557

Sign up for free and join Melanie's, and her brother, Simon Brown's, macrobiotic group at http://health.groups.yahoo.com/group/moderndaymacrobiotics/. Enjoy lively discussions, advice and recipe exchange.

Index

Please note that the recipes in plain text relate to a specific ingredient.

CPSIA information can be obtained at www.ICGtesting.com
Printed in the USA
266816BV00001B/6/P